"Christine Johnson puts the secret to taking charge of your life right in the palm of your hand. *Walk the Rainbow* is a book that helps you to accept the fact that you've got the power to make things happen in your life. Dr. Johnson provides a simple set of plans to put you in control of your world."

—Pauline Kimber, Editor/Co-Founder
CALIFORNIA ADVOCATE (Newspaper)

"For all those who believe their dream has been left by the wayside, for those who have been holding their breath waiting for success to happen, or for those who have said, 'poor me,' Christine Johnson offers this rebuttal: *Walk the Rainbow—When You Get Tired of Waiting to Exhale*. Written on the premise that you have the right to personal fulfillment, *Walk the Rainbow* presents the 'case' for you to take charge of your own life. As you read the book, the evidence is made available to you and the path to your personal rainbow is revealed."

—Honorable Ivy Glover Roberts, Administrative Law Judge

"*Walk the Rainbow* is an inspirationally adventuresome book... that assesses, stimulates, and invigorates you to become aware of your... potential. The message contained in the book will help you to see the various ways to attain personal success. It is an excellent resource book and a valuable contribution to the literature on the market."

—Eric Don-Pedro, Ph.D., Psychologist, Founder and CEO
WRIGHTLYNE CENTER FOR RESEARCH, TRAINING AND DEVELOPMENT

Walk the Rainbow

When You Get Tired of Waiting to Exhale

A "Right to" Book to Personal Fulfillment

CHRISTINE JOHNSON

A portion of this work was originally published in the December 17–31, 1994, issue of the *East Texas Ebony Journal*.

Book Design by White Light Publishing, Huntington Beach, California

Published by Sido-Mari Publishing, Huntington Beach, California

Printed in the United States of America

10 9 8 7 6 5 4 3 2 1

Library of Congress Cataloging-in-Publication Data

Johnson, Christine
Walk the Rainbow—When You Get Tired of Waiting to Exhale / Christine Johnson
p. cm
ISBN 0-9642257-4-3
1. Self Improvement 2. Success 3. Inspirational I.Title
94-092216
CIP

WE BLACK WOMEN
are the single group in the West intact.
And anybody can see we're pretty shaky.
We are, however (all praises),
the only group that derives its identity
from itself.

—Nikki Giovanni

Contents

Acknowledgments

I CONSIDER IT A BLESSING to be able to express my appreciation and gratitude to the following people:

- My sons Ralph and Roderic Bessard for their unconditional faith, encouragement, and "Atta Mama's."
- My sister Ella Lumpkin for her support and motivation throughout this project.
- Joan Haley and Jane Mejia for their commitment to the idea of walking the rainbow with me.
- My sister Willie Combs, brother Elgie Johnson, and friend Rosylin Bessard, who from the very beginning believed that I could write this book.
- My editor, Sharon Goldinger, for her understanding and persistence.
- Eric Don-Pedro for convincing me that the first step in writing the book was putting my thoughts on paper.
- All the "Sisters" who enriched my experiences by sharing with me. You know who you are.

To my parents

Odis and Mary Johnson.

Thank you for the dream and

the passion to pursue it.

Introduction

Comments from the Heart

Do you want to go through life waiting to exhale—only half alive? Many of us are doing exactly that, sitting around waiting for someone or something to make life meaningful and fulfilling. You have the right to walk the rainbow and enjoy life to its fullest. Walking the rainbow is a process by which a sister becomes the person she truly wants to be.

There is no simple or easy path to achieving personal fulfillment. Once you understand and acknowledge this fact, however, you can begin your journey on the path to personal fulfillment. This book will help you write your own declaration of independence in pursuit of happiness and personal fulfillment.

Walk the Rainbow is about those very private thoughts African American women carry around in their heads; it's about a woman's long quest for personal expression and creativity, her paradigm of self, what she thinks she can do, and how she envisions herself being the best she can be. It is a book about a woman's right to eliminate self-inflicted debilities that grow, develop, deceive, change, and engulf her in a personal paralysis.

In this book, I reach out and talk to you as if we are sitting across from each other at our mother's kitchen table, encouraging you to make meaningful choices and find right alternatives to the challenges you face in life.

The theme of this book is a sister's right to have whatever she desires from life. The book is laced with a basic assumption: an individual is responsible for what happens in her future, no matter what has happened in her past. The concepts imparted in the pages ahead will help you understand that you are unique, revealing to you that the one thing that you can do better than anyone else is be yourself. The book is a teaching and learning tool. It will compel you to take spontaneous action: take charge of your life and do not wait to exhale.

I have attempted to write this book from an experiential perspective as opposed to using a style that may be viewed as descriptive or prescriptive. Unlike some of the other advice books on the market, the information in this book will not leave you hanging—solutions to life's challenges are identified and resolved.

It took me years to reach the point where I could openly appreciate myself as a valuable human being. Reading this book will enable you to see the value in yourself and empower you to take control of whatever is happening around you. You will sense the vital role you play in determining and reaching your goals in life.

All too often we have allowed our lives to become boring, dull, and repetitious. The ideas presented in *Walk the Rainbow* will identify and demonstrate ways for you to create new situations and become a more effective person, more alive and exciting to yourself and others. The time and energy you put into understanding the concepts offered in this book will have many payoffs, both in your own life experience and your opportunities to enhance the experiences of others. As you progress with your walk over the rainbow, you will move into new dimensions of thinking, where living becomes increasingly exciting and new. You will have a new attitude toward yourself and the world in general.

Walk the Rainbow—When You Get Tired of Waiting to Exhale offers you a variety of alternatives to help shape your destiny instead of waiting for an external force to shape it for you. You can have an exciting and rewarding life by discovering a path to personal fulfillment.

It will be no great revelation for you to learn that the topics I have chosen to write about are ones I personally have been concerned with for a great deal of my adult life: (1) my quest or walk to establish my identity and (2) questions about life and external relationships.

Throughout my adult life I have met and interacted with sisters who have been struggling with the pain of finding the right balance for a productive life. It seemed easy for them to identify the problems, but more times than not the solutions were few and far between. The common thread found in many of our conversations was the control we allowed others to have over our lives.

I assume that you may have questions as you read this book. To respond to them and fulfill my own need to facilitate a better understanding of the personal empowerment ideas contained in this book, I have created seven fictional characters (Claudia, Julia, Sheila, Barbara, Dorothy, Paula, and Shirley) who interact with each other and move you through the basic empowerment concepts in the book. This approach allows you to look at personal success and fulfillment through the eyes of some people doing the living. *Walk the Rainbow* is a "right to" book that serves as a positive-living guide that will enable you to put your personal power to work for you every day. In other words, *Walk the Rainbow* is just plain, old-fashioned common sense.

A right to book does not have to be heavily laden with therapeutic principles to be effective. I have made a very deliberate effort to keep this book relevant to the feelings and speculations sisters experience on a daily basis. In Chapter 6, "The Principles in Action," the fictitious Claudia tells you the story of herself and her six female friends. Through the dialogues that take place in four sessions, we share their personal fulfillment journey across the rainbow.

When I started the book, I was writing for African American women. However, after I finished, I discovered that *Walk the Rainbow* is good for all who may have questions about who they are, how they arrived at where they are now in their lives, and where they want to go with the rest of their lives. There are many ways to use this book:

- as a nitty-gritty source of information to set and accomplish goals.
- as a method to identify stumbling blocks that may be preventing you from developing your full potential.
- as a way to recreate your lifestyle in a way that will allow you to express your true feelings in positive ways.

You decide how it will benefit you.

By now you know that I wrote this book to help myself. I hope the concepts in the book will also help other women walk their personal rainbow—reach their goals in life. The reward is your own personal fulfillment.

Chapter 1

How I Developed My Plan to Walk the Rainbow

I Stopped Doing the Things I Used to Do

When I decided that I wanted to change my life, I stopped doing the things I used to do—things that got in the way of my making positive changes in my life. I realized that if I didn't break old habits and take the first step, I would not get what I expected from life. This statement is a simple fact. Many sisters just like you are sitting around waiting to exhale before they experience life to the fullest. The *real* truth is that they will probably be in the same spot ten years from now if they don't take the first step. For a long time I sat around with the hundreds of "fixing-to" sisters who were waiting for the right moment to do something constructive with their lives. Ten years later, I was in the same fixing-to state. The things I used to do, like sitting around waiting, I do not do anymore. I deserve better.

In my personal quest for expression and creativity, it became evident to me that I needed to start my walk toward reaching my goals. As may be true for many of you, my goals were probably somewhat linked to the amount of gold I had in the bank. I am not talking about superficial riches; I am talking about taking care of the basics for me and the people who depend on me. I am talking about not being one or two paychecks from poverty, taking a vacation without having to count pennies, or having to rob Penny to pay Paula.

It became clear that I needed some help—a sense of direction. I also learned that if I was ever going to achieve anything beyond my present existence, I needed a plan.

As a successful and popular college administrator, I had the opportunity to come in contact with a large number of sisters who spent years in professional roles taking care of other people's lives. Very little time was devoted to preparing for their own futures. After observing many of these women, I finally started to pay attention to what was happening in my own life. My personal life was a joke. I did a lot for other people but did very little planning to promote a positive personal relationship. I determined that I was not alone in putting things off for myself. I knew of a number of successful sisters who never got around to planning their personal lives.

It also became obvious to me that while we plan small things like where we will go on vacation, what we will wear to a girlfriend's wedding, or who we will or will not sleep with, we leave to chance something as important as the rest of our lives. What is wrong with this picture? It's that most of us are just not accustomed to making plans for ourselves.

I decided to change all that. My plan was to participate in life to the fullest. I started to believe that there really is no limit to the fulfillment I can enjoy because there is no limit to the great inheritance from our Creator. I embraced a personal empowerment philosophy that told me that at the end of the rainbow there was a pot of "goal." Moreover, my new belief system told me that to obtain the pot of "goal" was my right in life and that I personally had to exercise that right.

I Created My Own Opportunities

I was almost fifty years old before I reached back and started to use some of the good old-fashioned common sense my parents tried to teach me. It seems that in the process of getting an education, I unlearned some of the values my parents taught me—for example, seeing myself as valuable. In my daily life I constantly struggled with internal and external challenges that mitigated my self-esteem. I raised two sons by myself. They were three and four years old when I divorced their father. During the years of building a career and being a single mother, I developed quite an attitude because I did not feel I was getting any breaks. As a matter of fact, there were times when circumstances seemed so bad that I did not think I could buy a break, even if I had the money.

Sometimes I would look around and, from my twisted perspective, others seemed to have passed me by. I would ask myself questions. Why do I have to struggle with life so? Am I not entitled to life's riches and rewards? Why is the good always gravitating toward other people? Why doesn't much of anything positive seem to be coming my way? What is wrong with me? Why haven't I met "Mr. Right?"—someone who could come along and have the resources to take me away from the hassles of everyday life. (You know, like they do in the movies.)

I was constantly telling myself that no matter what I did I wasn't making much progress. Somehow though I told myself that I would try one last time to get myself out of the rut. If it didn't work that time, I would just throw in the towel. I needed a break. Something in my world needed to change.

When I was going through these years, I did not realize that the only thing that needed to change was me. I was not sophisticated enough to see that the answer really had always been available to me. Finally, I realized that I had to create my own opportunities in life.

I bet that a lot of this dialogue sounds familiar to you. When I stopped and looked at my situation, I was able to see that I had to take responsibility for the answers to my questions and dissatisfaction with life. Just before I knocked on the door of fifty, I learned to fix things for myself.

First I asked myself, "Girlfriend, who are you? How do you see yourself? What do you see when you look in the mirror? Do you even know where you are going or why you are trying to get there? Why are you sitting around waiting for life to happen to you?"

I must tell you that when I first started asking myself these questions, there were times that I broke down and cried like a baby. I guess it was good that I was living alone because I am sure that any other adult would have thought I was crazy. I certainly thought that I was losing it several times.

My sons were so young that they did not understand what was happening with me. Occasionally when they would inquire, I would lie and tell them that the tears were a way for mommies to wash the dirt out of their eyes.

Now that they are both adults, we often talk about the early years. They tell me that less and less dirt seems to be getting into my eyes. Or they ask if I have found a new way of getting rid of it. My response to them is that the bifocals serve as a retardant to the dirt. Of course, the "yeah right" feedback from them tells me that maybe they do not believe me after all.

I Conducted a Personal Soul Search

I hope you don't think that I am suggesting that you beat yourself up about your present life. Maybe your life doesn't need fixing at all. If that is the case, I'm happy for you. But if there is something that needs changing or improving, this might be a good time to do it. It is more like I am saying, "Take a look at yourself."

I had to take a look at my self-image and do some very heavy-duty soul searching. I was forced to examine my own goals. I got very basic and even examined my personal and financial assets and liabilities. In the process of doing this soul searching, I discovered something about myself: that I was not using my talents to my advantage. This soul searching also revealed that I had placed restrictions upon myself. I looked myself right in the eye and forced myself to see the real me, which then led me to examine my paradigm of self and my basic lifestyle.

The frustration and stagnation that I was experiencing in my life were a reflection of how I saw myself in relation to the world around me. I realized I had to face myself in the mirror. I came to grips with the fact that it was my right to walk the rainbow—experience personal fulfillment.

Confronting and understanding oneself is not as hard as it first seems, I soon found out. After all, I had been around myself all of my life. But I was afraid that in the process I would lose the self that I had created—the self that I had grown accustomed to over the years, the self that I showed other people and believed they had grown to appreciate and depend on. Was I wrong! The truth is that like most of us, I had the tendency to resist any personal change.

I believe that we feel this way because we are so busy creating change among other people and straining for their approval in return. Most of us don't confront ourselves because we feel too uncomfortable doing so.

Unfortunately, we have grown accustomed to defining ourselves in terms of what we do for other people and not in terms of what we do for ourselves. In most cases, we cannot easily explain why we even do the things we do. I could not, and many of the sisters I know made themselves nervous wrecks living to please other people.

One such case concerned a sister, Faye Brown, who is a prominent attorney in Dallas.

> Faye is a member of a half-dozen boards, is active in several prestigious black women and civic organizations, and works with the NAACP. She is even a member of the board of directors for the private black college from which she graduated. She is actively being recruited to run for public office. She prides herself in being involved in both the black and white communities. Faye's explanation of the intensity of her

> involvement is that she has to be involved and able to "cross over" into both communities in order to be truly acceptable in either. Her schedule frequently gets so overloaded that she is forced to schedule appointments with her husband and teenage daughter several weeks ahead of schedule and then pray that she will not have to cancel. Once she laughingly told me that her daughter had spent two weeks at her grandmother's before she realized the daughter was not in the house. She said this was possible because the computer and the fax machine had become popular modes of communication for her family. Her three to four drinks a week long ago turned into three or four a day. She fondly talked about how she believed that she could drink all of the men in the law firm under the table. Faye is the first and only black woman to work in the law firm and views herself as being privileged to be allowed to work at the firm. She has been known to say that she will be a partner in the firm or die trying.

Faye has decided her path. She can continue in this direction and self-destruct or she can change. Some of you may be on a similar destructive path. If that is the case, ask yourself why and do something constructive about it. Conduct your own personal soul search.

When I started to examine my own frustration with life, I could see that much of my frustration involved what I actually had in life rather than what I felt about myself. In my private moments, I was able to articulate my observations about what others were doing without even giving much thought about my specific personal wants and desires. During my soul searching, I realized that if I was ever going to be able to change my course in life, I had to change the way I was conducting my personal affairs. Just like a traveler getting ready for a trip needs a road map of where she is going, I had to develop a map for what I wanted to do with the rest of my life.

I Stopped Singing the Blues

I could not start my walk over the rainbow until I stopped singing the blues and became willing to find solutions to some very basic problems within myself. When I started looking at myself, I realized that I was suffering from something I labeled the "Dependent Woman Blues." I called it that because in my efforts to be everything to everybody, I had stopped being who I wanted to be. This was a good name for my attitude because what I wanted to be at the time was dependent on others' attitudes toward me while I showed people what they wanted to see—that the real me was someone completely different from what the public and my friends saw when they interacted with me. With this action, I created a third self—a shadow self: a self that was always singing the blues about what was wrong with my life but taking no responsibility to change it. In the long run, the third self ended up being the real me—the self that was uniquely me but somehow had become intertwined with makeovers and have-tos shaped by other people's perceptions.

Finally, I realized that my walk over the rainbow would be different from anyone else's. I came to understand that how I saw myself was dependent upon my distorted self-awareness at that time. It was through this awareness that I was expressing myself to the world. As may be true for many of you, my self-image, what I felt and saw in my mirror, was probably a reflection of where and how I saw myself in relation to my world. Mostly, I compared myself with my affluent friends. I matched my skills, abilities, talents, and aptitudes with those of other sisters around me. It is interesting that I never compared myself to white women. My sisters were my yardsticks.

I was constantly beating myself up and tearing myself apart. As a single woman, I became the one-woman trio: the career woman, the mother, the community social worker.

I sincerely believed that I had to be the best at all of these; otherwise, I was a failure.

During my brief marriage, I imagined and imposed a script on both my husband and myself that was so unrealistic no two human beings could play it out. I expected picture-show perfect behavior and romance. What happened was quite different. Since my husband was not living up to my unrealistic expectations, I viewed him as mistreating me. I went through a period of thinking my husband alone was making the marriage dysfunctional. "Mama, He Treats Your Daughter Mean" could have been a perfect theme song for the way I viewed my marriage. But, because in my eyes I was not living up to my expectations either, I did not see myself as deserving of any better treatment. Thus, I became the victim.

Fortunately, with time I came to understand that our expectations of each other were not realistic. Neither of us was prepared for the psychological and social aspects of being married. Not knowing what to do or even who to ask for help, I got out of the marriage too quickly to validate the quality of the relationship. Years would pass before I took an objective look at the guilt I placed upon myself for not making my marriage work. It was also a long time before I realized that bitterness had built up inside me and prevented me from having meaningful relationships after my divorce.

Not too long ago, I talked with my ex-husband about our marriage. Surprisingly, I learned from him that he viewed *himself* as the guilty party and responsible for the failure of the marriage. You know, a strange thing happens when people start to communicate with each other—sometimes they reach an understanding. My ex-husband and I reached that understanding twenty years too late.

There was nothing magical about the way I started to make progress. I looked at my self-imposed expectations. I had placed other people's aspirations and expectations above my own. These self-imposed expectations were intricately linked to my feelings of self-esteem. I also learned that within myself these expectations helped label my successes and define my failures.

My feelings of self-worth and self-devaluation developed from a social and cultural framework. My social and cultural environment shaped my self-image and behaviors and governed my interactions with the world around me. If a particular behavior received a positive response from family, friends, and the public, then this behavior was perfected and used when appropriate. Conversely, if the behavior was received negatively, then it would not be repeated for fear of losing face and acceptance. I learned to play the game, and I was good at it.

After my divorce, I also went through years of feeling like a social misfit. I isolated myself, even from my own feelings. I showed my family and friends only what I thought they wanted to see from me. What they saw was a sister who had dissolved a difficult marriage without any visible scars. The real situation was a sister who pretended to have all the answers and was lost in the deception. Having been born and raised in the rural South, my lifestyle at that time contradicted my expectations regarding marriage and family and the values I imposed upon myself. While the world around me changed in the seventies and relaxed its standards, I continued to place greater restrictions on my own behavior. To the detriment of my psychological and social well-being, I continued to act out the unrealistic expectations of my youth and to function according to what I believed others expected of me. Living up to what I thought was expected of me, I created the strong sister image for myself without developing the psychological support to back up my career woman and single parent roles. Consequently, my briefcase stayed full of the blues all the time. I was engaged in a no-win war with myself.

It became clear to me that in order for me to change, I had to change the way I interacted within my social and cultural environment. I had to learn ways to preserve and protect myself from the devaluing situations I had helped to create.

This is not an easy task in the African American community and is especially difficult for African American women because our social and business worlds sometimes overlap and contradict each other. Like other African American women, I usually defined myself from a multifaceted perspective.

This type of definition, without any real detailed exploration of who I was as a person, created problems for me. I had numerous roles (mother, educator, leader, friend, loved one). But who was I really? You see, when I went through the process of answering that question, there was not much I could conceal from myself. At first, I ran hard from the answer. My expectations of myself were ridiculous. No one person could possibly be and do all of the things I demanded of myself. My true self was locked somewhere deep within me, smothered and stagnated for a long time. The person I had allowed myself to become very skillfully barricaded the door to my true being for many years. I went on for years working against the gentle, unheeded urging of my inner voice until slowly but surely the created self got the best of my self-esteem.

This made it hard for me to truly appreciate myself even though I had a successful career and had successfully raised my sons. I was not able to solve my problems because I did not consciously acknowledge that I had any. It was difficult for me to see myself as valuable because I was so fragmented.

I Accepted Myself

Most of us view ourselves the way we think society views us. Some of the frustration we may experience on a daily basis could be largely dependent on self-imposed restrictions. Before I could change my life, I stopped and asked myself if my personal expectations were realistic and whether I accurately interpreted the expectations of others. The responses to these questions were critical for my developing the right perspective toward my life. When it finally came time for me to stop putting off making a decision, I was the one sitting around whining about life and waiting to exhale.

I believe that before any personal growth can take place, a realistic look in the mirror is imperative. That look helped me to first confront and then accept myself. I was ready to see what was reflected back at me without running away and without denial.

I found that I was the one placing stigmas and restrictions on myself for being whatever I thought I was or was not. My children long ago accepted the fact that I was divorced from their father. In fact, they seemed to have enjoyed having two homes, two summer vacations, and two sets of holidays.

Self-acceptance did not come easily for me. For a period of time, I wrestled with the concept that personal understanding and self-acceptance come from staying focused on who you are and conducting your life on your own terms. This concept was difficult for me to grasp because I was so accustomed to doing for others first and then for myself. My preoccupation with pleasing others distracted me from accepting myself. I had to learn the importance of determining my own direction in life. Gradually, it became clear to me that if I accepted myself, I would be in a great position to determine my future. The path to reaching self-acceptance comes in focus when you understand that.

Self-acceptance is many things—it is multidimensional. It consists of your beliefs, ideas, attitudes, experiences, and feelings. It is feeling or seeking expression. All of these ideas are on a continuum that moves from your deepest self to outer expression and fulfillment. Self-acceptance is reaching the point when you understand that all of these ideas are important aspects of your life. When self-acceptance happened, it was quite revealing for me to find out that nothing was holding me back in life except my thoughts and the limitations I imposed on my own mind and my own actions. I learned that how we perceive ourselves can change. I believe if a stubborn-minded person like me can change, anyone can. This is the basic premise of this book.

The perception you hold of yourself can change by altering conditions both inside and outside of yourself. It goes without saying that these changes can be for the better or for the worse. Until I decided to take charge of my life, the changes in my life always seemed to be for the worse. This was because of my limited viewpoint toward life. I saw things as happening *to* me instead of me making things happen *for* me. There is a huge gap between the two ideas.

Part of this attitude was understandable because women of color in general have to wrestle with the real boundaries of the social and cultural challenges of racism and sexism. When I started accepting myself, I realized that I wanted to do something different with my life. No one else could take this responsibility for me.

When I started my self-acceptance campaign, I realized that I wanted to do something about the way I looked and felt about myself. I also decided that no longer would I be the victim of "quick fixes." This time I would really look at myself and stop feeling sorry about everything that was not the way I wanted it to be. I would change things that needed to be or could be changed. The rest of the mess I would leave for a higher authority to handle.

With this revelation came a new understanding of change itself. I realized that change can be for both the short term and/or the long term. What you see in yourself can be real or imagined. The way you behave is usually consistent with what you perceive to be true about yourself or about your circumstances.

I began to see that I had a number of sources constantly telegraphing information into my psyche. But with my new understanding, the only messages I would pay attention to were those I wanted to hear for myself. For a long time, I was unable to reject the bitter and incorporate the sweet into my daily life. After I truly accepted myself, I was able to see that life can be difficult and the inherent peaks and valleys are a natural part of it.

It was difficult for me to understand that all people are not created equal. People are individuals, no matter what you want to believe. Early in life we buy into the American dream that we are all created equal. This is a very misleading and frustrating fallacy. I believe that we are all equal in God's eyes, but in reality many people do not always see it that way. They sometimes ask the question, "What happened to my share of the American dream?" Some people feel that they get left out when equality is being handed out. For a long time I felt that way.

As basic as this might sound, I did not understand the idea of equality. If we were all equal, then we should have the same accomplishments, same objectives, and same attitudes. But experience told me this wasn't the case. The simple fact is we are not equal. However, realizing that everyone has an equal opportunity to take responsibility for his or her life helped me look at things differently. I was able to see that I was wrong for trying to incorporate someone else's views into my own life. I finally accepted the truth—there is no one else like me on the face of this Earth. I finally stopped chasing other people's rainbows and started to cast myself according to the script I wanted to write for my own life.

Too many of us go through life trying to identify as a group of women instead of as individuals. Everyone does not have to wear the same designer clothes, have the same hair cut, and shop at the same overpriced stores to be a bona fide African American woman. Now that I understand it is acceptable for African American women to be different from each other, I have stopped worrying about these differences. Even though we may be of the same race, there are a number of differences we have to keep in the top of our minds at all times, including backgrounds, heritage, and intelligence, and they all differ from one to the next. Sometimes the only things that stand between a sister and her fulfilled life are her perception of these differences and the will and faith she needs to keep going.

Historically, African American women have demonstrated intense faith and will and the strength to surmount seemingly impossible odds and obstacles. Ironically, perhaps it is this strength that may be blocking present-day fulfillment. When I accepted myself and fully understood my own strengths as a person, I was able to truly take charge of my own life, and it felt so good.

Chapter 2

We All Can Walk the Rainbow

Transform from Aunt Jemima to Ain't Your Mama

For whatever reason, a significant number of sisters have learned to inhibit the expression of their true feelings. They put the feelings of others before their own personal interests and needs. Many of us have not learned how to enthusiastically accept ourselves as valuable human beings. However, if we want others to view us as valuable, we must take the lead and declare and accept ourselves. We have to stop seeing the sky as raining despair and see it as showering hope.

Today if we are not very careful, we could become so overwhelmed by what is wrong in our community that we could relinquish all hope for the future. The problems could simply quash a sister's motivation to keep the faith. Every way she turns she is confronted with another problem to solve. How does she handle the complex personal and social problems constantly being dumped unsolicited into her lap?

With the deterioration of the black family, the fragmentation of the black community, and the incarceration of the black man, who will revere the black woman? How will she get and maintain her motivation for life? I have come to believe that the first step may well be for the African American woman to assume the role of her own advocate.

It is obvious to me that women who succeed in life show enthusiasm for living. It makes me so sad to see young twenty-year-old sisters dragging their tails through life—looking hopeless and helpless, with self-esteem so low they can sweep the street with it. Before these women will ever be able to do anything truly and lastingly positive for themselves, they have to transform their attitude. They have to stop internalizing their burdens before they can do something constructive for themselves, changing from an Aunt Jemima to an ain't-your-mama attitude.

I describe the Aunt Jemima attitude as the belief that you have to be the caretaker for everyone else before you look out for yourself. Conversely, the ain't-your-mama attitude allows you to care for yourself first, enabling you to serve humanity at a much more dignified level.

For a long time, I held the belief that I had to be not only the caretaker for my family but also be responsible for everyone else in Mr. Rogers' neighborhood who needed a helping hand. This Aunt Jemima complex is manifested in a lot of African American women out there who have the one-woman trio blues. These women single-handedly take on community, family, and world responsibilities before doing for themselves.

When the behavior prompted by the Aunt Jemima complex persists, we start to see ourselves as victims. In time, this behavior becomes a horrible habit that definitely has its downside.

Personally, it was difficult for me to shake the Aunt Jemima attitude. I had to cross over to a new way of thinking. The new attitude said "I ain't your mama" and helped deliver me to a different level of thinking. No longer did I feel the need to be everyone's caretaker. Gradually, I was able to let other people assume their fair share of responsibility for themselves.

Sisters who are successful in life show you that they accept and love themselves. They demonstrate their self-confidence by their attitudes and behaviors. Some sisters experience difficulty in appreciating the distinction between self-confidence and egotism because we are taught from a very early age to suppress our egos and be humble. There comes a time in all of our lives when we must decide to develop the self-confidence and take control over our lives. This can be done without being egotistical.

I have learned a lot from other sisters by watching them walk and talk to each other. You could say that I became a sister watcher. I like to watch confident African American women declare their attitude toward life by the way they walk. I especially like to watch women who by their behavior and mannerisms appear to have read and internalized Maya Angelou's *Phenomenon Woman*. No other woman can walk like a confident sister. Her walk tells her story—where she's been and where she's going. The tired sister also tells her story in her walk.

There are a lot of together African American women who could be viewed as role models. Whenever I found myself slipping back into that "somebody done me wrong" attitude, I did an about-face and remembered some of the outstanding contributions African American women have made in this world. This type of vicarious "atta girl" worked for me.

One of the major characteristics of a woman who has accepted herself is that she builds upon her basic strengths. African American women have innate basic strengths. African heritage tells us not to see ourselves as victims. The contemporary victimization attitude demonstrated by many of our young sisters is a new phenomenon that is out of line with the teachings of African heritage—the legacy that as African Americans you are descendants of kings and queens, heiresses to the riches and abundance of the universe.

Acquisition of the ain't-your-mama attitude frees you to become a positive caretaker of your own personal needs. It takes the victimization mentality away so that you accept yourself as a valuable and worthwhile woman. Sisters who have accepted themselves establish and maintain positive mental attitudes consistent with the African heritage image. These women also understand that habit-breaking is very difficult. But they stay focused on what they want and they don't stop until they accomplish their goals.

It is important to remember that the difference between the degree of success of a woman who has accepted herself and the woman who has not is largely a matter of attitude. All my life I have heard people say that a person's attitude can make or break her. A sister's attitude depends upon what she believes to be true about herself. She must believe that she can do whatever she wants to do. She would be well served to keep in mind what Napoleon Hill said, "What the mind can conceive and believe it can achieve."

Kill Sapphire—She Is Alive But She Ain't Well

We hear the word "attitude" every day. It is a word discussed in every profession. We talk about it at home, at work, at parties, and yes, in bed. I believe that no other word will have more influence on your life or future than attitude. This is true because your attitude is your greatest asset. It can also be your greatest liability. From a social and cultural perspective, African Americans historically have been forced to wear the onerous "jacket of negative attitudes." Other phrases commonly associated with a bad attitude include "chip on the shoulder" and the "Sapphire" image.

If you have a chip on your shoulder, it is time for you to shake it off. The chip is too burdensome to carry and serves no purpose. The Sapphire stereotype portrays the African American woman as Bible-toting, foulmouthed, obese, indefatigable at work, insatiable in bed, and a prolific breeder. If you're acting like Sapphire, it's time to kill her off. I believe that the Sapphire image has betrayed us sisters. Society in general is all too comfortable with laying the burdens of the entire black race at the Sapphire sisters' feet.

A real sapphire is a jewel capable of sparkling and bringing great joy into the lives of others. See yourself as that sapphire—a precious jewel. Then kill off the old stereotypical Sapphire. She has been using you and pulling you down long enough. You have no use for her anymore. This is the one time that you will see me openly advocating mercy killing. Put Sapphire out of her misery; get her off the life support system. Let her die peacefully. You know she is ready to go. May God have mercy on her soul.

I understand that Sapphire was not really responsible for the role she had to play. When I listen to the concerns of sisters all over the country, they tell me that the Sapphire image is just too heavy for them to carry. They want some relief and say that the best way to obtain the desired relief is to let Sapphire go ahead and die. With the Sapphire image dead and gone, sisters tell me that when they get tired they can sit down and rest. They are no longer held hostage by this terrible image. When they feel discouraged, they can express it without a negative label. If you have a problem with leaving the Sapphire image behind, ask yourself, "What has the Sapphire image ever done for me?"

If your attitude is positive or bright, your life will reflect this. While you may not move through life with the ease of a gazelle, generally speaking, you will be a happy person. On the other hand, if you demonstrate a negative attitude, you will probably find numerous obstacles in your path. Many doors will be closed to you, and your walk through life will be blocked. If I were a betting person, I would bet that your personal life would be so much more fun, so much more fulfilling, with a good attitude.

If the things you used to do are beneficial to you, then keep on doing them. Do not let anyone dictate what your attitude should be—you have to make the final call regarding your behavior.

Your mental state determines how you will respond to people, places, circumstances, and things. If you have not done so already, take time to examine your attitude. If your attitude is not consistent with the image you want to project, change your attitude. For example, if you were getting dressed for work or a social function and the outfit you planned to wear suddenly did not seem to be the right color or fit, you would probably change into something more appropriate and pleasing. You can do the same with your attitude.

> I am reminded of Luanne Jones, a woman I met a few years ago, who insisted on portraying a Sapphire attitude. She was always angry and dominated relationships and situations with verbal abuse and frequent manipulations. When she spoke about her perceptions of life, she would project the world as cruel and the people in it as uncaring. She perceived most people as her enemy, and the few who she viewed as friends were constantly subjected to ridicule. When she decided to confront herself, it was not long before she realized that she had done nothing to establish and maintain positive relationships with others. The result of her attitude was fewer and fewer friends. Through the act of self-acceptance, she was able to grow as a person and gradually learned to accept other people as well.

Like Luanne, your attitude extends to all facets of your life. You have an attitude toward clothes, cars, lifestyles, and people around you. It is important for you to realize that you have a choice about your attitude toward life. You can decide to put all your energy on the negative aspects of your life. On the other hand, you can focus your attention on the positive aspects of your world. The choice is up to you. One thing is certain: you do not have to sit around waiting to exhale.

Learn When It Is Time to Dust Your Broom

There comes a time when you must make a decision to go forward, go backward, or stagnate. It was not until recently that the time came for me to move in the direction

I wanted my life to go. The years were passing and I was still fixing to do my thing—whatever that was at the time.

In the South where I grew up, the old folks had a saying for when a conversation was over or reached a point where no one was going to win, "I believe I'll dust my broom." My grandmother used to get even more basic when she had finished talking with people and they had just left her home. Picture her as I saw her then, a petite, small-framed woman, paper-sack tan skin, no visible wrinkles even though she was nearly seventy, rigidly erect posture, and surefooted in her every movement. Every evening, just before bedtime, grandmother used to get her broom and sweep the dirt in front of the steps. When she finished this ritual, she would dust her broom vigorously.

As a young girl growing up, I asked my grandmother about the significance of this activity. She responded, "The day is done, ain't nothing else happening around here tonight. Tomorrow ain't here yet, ain't no need leaving these tracks up in here for you and me to deal with tomorrow. Dust 'em out the way tonight, make it easy for you and me to get started tomorrow."

It took me almost fifty years to understand that there is much to be learned from my grandmother's ritual. I learned how to leave yesterday's dirt in the past. There was no need for me to carry yesterday's problems into tomorrow. I also learned that there is a time and place to dust the broom and we each have to figure out when that time arrives. We have to know when we have reached that point when "ain't nothing else happening" with the situation. You could say that it is making right choices at the right time. Trust me, there really does come a time to dust the broom. Forget about yesterday's tracks and take giant steps forward. No half steps will do. Dust them out of the way today and make it easy for yourself to get started tomorrow.

The world we live in has both positive and negative aspects competing for our attention. Many people operate from the perspective that life experiences are either negative or positive. When you have this attitude toward life, you have no middle ground. Unfortunately, for many years I let too many negative thoughts monopolize my life. I'm over that now. You can get past it, too, if you stop letting negative thoughts paralyze your behavior. The truth is that life is what we make of it and the foundation of a positive life is in the mind.

Les Brown, an internationally known motivational speaker, has the right idea. Basically, he has two rules about life. Rule Number One: Don't sweat the petty stuff. Rule Number Two: It is all petty stuff. At first this type of attitude may seem too frivolous, but if you think about it long enough, you will grasp his meaning. It means don't worry about things; worry never solves anything. Learn to detach yourself from problems and don't let them bury you.

I want you to think about Les Brown's rules for a moment, then look at your life from the perspective of a stranger. Make a note of what you see. Find something positive even if you have to embellish it a little bit. Do this every day until you truly begin to feel positive and your actions reflect that feeling. After a short while, you will feel so good that you will never want to revert to your old way of thinking. If you already feel good about yourself or certain aspects of your life, look for other good things and you will begin to feel twice as good. Before long, the feeling becomes contagious.

Stop the Victimization

One of the aspects of taking control of your life and personal fulfillment is that the process depends largely on how you view the world. Keep in mind the idea that the world we live in has both the negative and positive always competing for your attention. But remember, you do have a choice about your perception of the world and the direction you take in life. You and only you can decide to choose the positive or negative road. For your own betterment, it is a good idea to establish a time to check out of the negative state of mind. However, if on any given day you choose to demonstrate your multifaceted personality and revert to Sapphire or Aunt Jemima, ain't nobody's business if you do. The difference now is that you decide which role suits you, and this is where it starts to feel good. You usually get out of life what you are looking for. A positive attitude is a natural manifestation of your new way of looking at life.

It may be necessary to examine the motives behind why some women continue to assume the role of victim. One such woman, Marva Calhoun, became known to me a few years ago.

> Marva was depressed when I met her at a church function. She told me that her husband was drinking heavily and both her teenage daughters got pregnant within months of each other and had dropped out of high school. Both the girls were still living at home when I met Marva. When I first started talking to her, she did not appear to see anything wrong with the situation in her home. In fact, she appeared to be very proud of her ability to take care of her family. During one of our conversations she said, "I have a twenty-four-hour, seven-day-a-week shift and it looks like I might be working myself into an early grave—but I have to take care of my family." Marva was a nurse at a local hospital and at the time was the only one in her family working. She was babysitting the two grandchildren all of the time even though she felt the girls should be putting forth more effort toward the care of the babies. Marva kept the bar at her home full of liquor even though she said she knew her husband had been drinking too much since he had been laid off from his job. She did not see how she could behave any differently toward her family because they needed her. Interestingly, after Marva began her walk over the rainbow, she gradually learned that she did not have to be everything to everybody to feel needed. She came to express her own needs and interests. She fostered interdependence in her daughters and moved them into an

> apartment of their own. They cared for their own children and alternated babysitting while the other was in school. She learned that her misguided love for her husband was not helping him or their marriage. He went back to school for retraining, and they both joined an at-risk couples support group at their church. The last time I saw Marva, she did not seem so depressed.

Contrary to what a large number of our grandmothers and mothers told us, our walk through life really can be joyous and predictable. I know that a lot of us grew up thinking that we had to suffer before we could be happy. Discard that idea now. We do not have to buy into this myth. We can measure our results as we step along the way.

Life does not have to be a repeat of no pain, no gain. Figuratively speaking, you can banish a cloudy day just by the way you think and feel about yourself. Remember, you can turn your stamina into something very positive. Stop the self-victimization. Look at the path others have traveled and discover that the happiest, most successful sisters seem to possess positive attitudes, characteristics, and habits.

Develop Self-Determination Skills

When I started my walk, I decided to look at lifestyle patterns of successful sisters. I discovered that successful women seem to possess the following five basic self-determination skills:

1. Successful women set themselves apart from the general population by being persistent in all of their endeavors. These women establish goals and remain steadfast in their efforts to achieve them. They do not quit until they have fulfilled their dreams.

2. Successful women take risks without fear of failure. They understand that nothing in life is guaranteed, and they

also know how to benefit from their past mistakes. They learn how to calculate risk as it relates to establishing and meeting their goals.

3. Successful women have vision—they see what is possible, not just what is. Sometimes we spend so much time living in the past that we do not know where we are going. Face it, girlfriend, you cannot see where you are going if you are busy looking backward. Do not let the past block your vision of the future. Successful sisters are able to visualize the seemingly impossible and make it happen in their own lives. They create positive conditions that make things happen for themselves instead of letting things happen to them.

4. Successful women possess strong self-esteem. They demonstrate that they believe in themselves by the way they remain focused on their own goals in life. This strong self-esteem serves as support when they encounter frustrating and challenging situations.

5. Successful women are optimistic. In other words, they stay tuned to the positive station by internalizing the FM (for me) instead of the AM (against me) attitude toward life. Keep in mind that the for-me attitude suggests that a woman knows and understands that it is her right to inherit the abundance of the universe. On the other hand, the against-me attitude portrays the idea that the sister believes she does not have the right to anything. Successful sisters celebrate their assets, not their liabilities. No more "pity parties" or "been there, done that" attitudes.

Your outlook on life determines when and how you will eventually walk the rainbow. In order to start the walk in life, you have to be optimistic about the future and your ability to create the future you desire. Let go of the barriers that have been obstructing your view of the rainbow. You can walk the rainbow anytime you are ready.

Chapter 3

Getting Ready for the Walk

Break Down Mental Barriers

Many sisters are concerned about finding a path to personal achievement and empowerment. It is a lot easier to learn something if your approach is systematic rather than haphazard. This part of the book offers insights for a systematic approach to accomplishing personal fulfillment—what I call walking the rainbow. This information prepares you for the walk over the rainbow and provides psychological perspectives that will help you focus on the task of accomplishing the walk.

An important skill that will be needed to get ready for the walk is your ability to focus your full attention on yourself. We seem to define ourselves in terms of the desires of other people. This idea of putting other people ahead of yourself gives you a convenient cop-out or excuse for not taking care of your own business the way you dreamed of or know you could. Set the excuses aside. It is time for you to take another step toward taking control of your life and achieving personal fulfillment.

The time has come for you to stop using what you do for other people as a barrier for not accomplishing your own goals. You have to train yourself to pay attention to your own needs. Ask yourself this question: "What else is standing in my way, if not me?"

Few of us have a magical or quick-fix answer to this question. To realistically get on course with our lives there are a few barriers that most of us have to eliminate before we can take a bold and self-fulfilling walk over the rainbow. Eliminating most if not all of the barriers before you begin the walk is extremely important. If you do not eliminate the barriers, you may find yourself taking one step forward and two steps backward. Or worse, you may find yourself getting sidetracked altogether and never getting back on course.

When I have talked with my African American sisters on various occasions, I have observed three basic barriers to staying focused on our goals. These barriers are probably not unique to African American women, so why am I mentioning them in this discussion? Some sisters have a tendency to think that we are the "only ones to" and "only ones who" experience what we are experiencing most of the time. Park that attitude and forget to go back for it.

Eliminate Barriers

Get started on the path to walking the rainbow by eliminating three major barriers.

The first barrier is "targeted apathy." I know some of you sisters will say that you are not apathetic. If that is not true for you, ignore the comment. Targeted apathy is not readily visible to the naked eye. In fact, some of us may still be in denial about our apathetic lifestyles.

The form of apathy I am talking about is highly addictive. It justifies your indifference by letting you think that what you are doing is important. This form of apathy can last a week, a month, a year, or even a lifetime because some parts of your life may still be moving in a very positive direction. In fact, too many of us sisters are very aggressive and even indefatigable about some aspects of our lives and painfully apathetic toward others.

Let us examine a few of the areas that are likely to surface as targeted apathetic patterns for sisters. What about fitness? I know this remains a particularly difficult aspect of my life and a tough barrier for me to break down.

I went through most of my thirties and early forties as an overweight, unhealthy person. I did this while I was accomplishing a number of other fantastic career objectives. This situation made me live in two worlds: the professional world where I felt comfortable and competent to hold my own and my private world where my self-esteem was very low. I denied to myself that being overweight interfered with my having a quality personal life. I told myself the reason my personal life was on hold was because I did not have time to develop meaningful relationships. The real truth is that I did not feel attractive and did not have any confidence about my worthiness to be loved by others.

It was not easy for me to admit this to myself. When I finally got strong enough to discuss my personal appearance with friends and relatives, some of them were so busy basking in my personal accomplishments that they too denied that I needed to do something about my weight. Another reason I did not feel compelled to do anything about my fitness program was because some of the people around me were more apathetic about their weight than I was. When I compared myself to them, I looked very forward-thinking and in some cases I did not look much out of shape.

Whenever you move toward changing bad habits, you learn to observe yourself from a different perspective and stop comparing yourself with others. For example, the conscious realization that I had to take charge of my life helped me make the decision to initiate a personal fitness program. But I had to develop ownership for myself before I could initiate actions to change my life. Personal empowerment allows you to see yourself as capable of taking charge of your own life while simultaneously neutralizing the power or control that others have over you.

Another area where some of us sisters could use a kick in the pants is our love life. Why do so many of us insist on holding on to dysfunctional relationships with our African

American brothers? Some sisters I know have a "do-nothing" attitude toward dumping bad relationships, and sometimes it is just too painful to watch. It remains a mystery to me why so many of us tend to let "going-nowhere-fast" relationships ruin our lives. These kinds of relationships can become toxic and nonproductive.

Here's an example. Improper storage of toxic waste in the environment is against the law. Sisters should take a look at how the government handles violators of the toxic waste laws; there are heavy penalties to pay. Therefore, the next time you get caught up in the trap of holding in toxic material, exhale it before it becomes life-threatening. It can also literally destroy your physical health and self-esteem. The same applies to toxic relationships. Why not dump them?

> My friend Carla Washington shares her home with her male cousin. She told me that one of her cousin's girlfriends called six times in the same evening to talk with him. The girlfriend said the reason she was calling was to tell him how awful he was for not keeping a date with her the evening before. The first three calls were displays of outrage. By the fourth call, the woman was asking for an explanation of his behavior. In the fifth call she was apologizing for not understanding his schedule and begging for forgiveness for the terrible things she said on the first three calls. By the time the sister made the sixth call, she was pathetically begging the brother to let her fix dinner for him the next night.
>
> Carla told me that this sister had been in this dysfunctional relationship with her cousin for over four years. When he got around to it, he would pay her a mercy visit and calm her down. Then the cycle would start all over again.

Carla's story is probably not an isolated example of how targeted apathy can be completely debilitating and demoralizing to the point that a person could become paralyzed. Unless the woman Carla told me about comes to grips with her own role in maintaining this pitiful relationship, she will never take the necessary steps to extricate herself and move forward with her life.

Targeted apathy has to be removed from your psyche if you are going to be successful in moving forward. Once you have made the commitment to do something, take a cue from Nike and "just do it." Do it with enthusiasm.

The second barrier or roadblock to overcome when you begin your walk over the rainbow is "episodic procrastination." This barrier is the favorite sister of apathy. When episodic procrastination teams up with targeted apathy against a person, the end result can be very destructive to the victim. Episodic procrastination can be very inviting and lull you into a comfortable web of stagnation. Consequently, it places no demands or expectations on you. I know a lot of high-potential sisters who got in bed with procrastination and never got up again.

Episodic procrastination has a split personality and operates with many disguises. The most common disguise is the illusion of being your friend and making you feel comfortable by keeping you company, which prevents you from being involved in meaningful activity. Trust me; this type of procrastination is not your friend. When procrastination knocks on your door and tells you that it is there to help, believe it just like you do the IRS. When it knocks, understand that it plans to stay awhile and you will pay dearly while it is there and long after it leaves.

Episodic procrastination is the opposite of movement. Therefore, overcoming it is extremely hard work. When fighting procrastination, be careful; it is very slick, smooth, tricky, and ruthless. Sometimes it appears as a best friend bringing good news. Sometimes it even appears as a telephone call or an inviting lover. No matter in what form it comes to you, it will get in the way of your doing what you need to do in order to keep moving toward your goals in life. Kill it off as soon as you recognize it for what it is. Have no mercy on this vile creature. Be patient with yourself, but don't give in. Like apathy, once you get caught in the web of procrastination, it is very difficult to break loose.

If you liked targeted apathy, you will love episodic procrastination. The addiction is not quite as apparent to others. Procrastination plays with your mind. It helps you play mental games with yourself. In too many cases, episodic procrastination gives you time to spend with other sisters at pity parties and by yourself languishing on the "pity pot." It goes out of its way to sabotage your goals and helps you identify excuses for why you need to delay implementing your plans.

Episodic procrastination convinces you that a state of paralysis or a fixing-to mentality is the place for you to be. It becomes your partner in waiting. You're not lonely; you have your best friend with you while you wait.

Procrastination is a very crippling disease. It is the greatest dream killer you are likely to face. One of the best ways to rid yourself of procrastination is to start your walk over the rainbow with small steps. Devote ten to fifteen minutes a day to doing something about your goals in life. Then slowly build up to at least thirty minutes a day, which will increase your productivity on a weekly basis.

The third barrier to walking the rainbow is "acquired negativity." Acquired negativity is highly destructive and will let you get caught up in a tight web that can be detrimental to your efforts toward accomplishing your goals. This type of negativity becomes a part of your thoughts over a period of time. It happens so gradually that in some cases you are not even aware that you have it. Take a giant step away from acquired negativity and leave negative thoughts behind you. Don't look back.

You and you alone must know when it is time to wage your war against the things in your life that may be holding you back. Your walk over the rainbow will not be productive if you bring your negatives with you. It is important for you to know that once you start the walk over the rainbow to fulfill your goals, you will need to eliminate negative thoughts. Negative thoughts keep you guessing and doubting your own capabilities and prevent you from accomplishing your goals. When you let acquired negativity stay in your thoughts, it gradually becomes self-fulfilling.

If you believe that you can't do something, then more than likely you will not do it. The formula is simple. If you think you can, you can. If you think you can't, you can't. Another thing to remember is that if you listen too long to negative people, this may cause you to think negative thoughts. My advice is to distance yourself from negative people. Most negative people are looking for other negative people. Remember the old adage "misery loves company." Choose not to provide the negative company. It is better for your walk over the rainbow if you deal with enthusiastic, positive people. Like you, these people will probably have a sense of direction and a plan of action on how to get where they want to go.

After you have eliminated the three barriers to your path, it is time to take the walk over the rainbow. What direction will you take? Just like you would not try to drive to an unfamiliar city without a road map, you don't start your walk over the rainbow without a sense of direction.

Change Stumbling Blocks to Steppingstones

When you select the road to travel in life, you have to overcome a number of obstacles. Don't get sidetracked with the "we-shall-overcome" attitude portrayed in the song during the Civil Rights movement. From my perspective, that song did not free anyone in the past and it ain't going to free nobody in the near future! The reason that some people who endorsed that song thirty years ago may still be singing it today could be that they probably did not pay much attention to the words. The concept [theme] of this song put everything in the future. "We shall overcome someday, I do believe… "

Well, maybe someday you will overcome, but what about today? What do you propose to do about your life or dreams this morning or this afternoon, not someday out in the uncertain future? This attitude has to be the epitome of the fixing-to mentality I talked about earlier. It is also a declaration of not having a specific goal to follow today. You cannot move forward talking about an abstract day in the future; you need a sense of direction—today.

Before starting the walk over the rainbow, you must select a realistic and practical goal. Picture it clearly in your mind; focus your thoughts on it and become enthusiastic about it. Use that active imagination of yours to visualize what you want in life. Select the road you want to travel. You will not be able to start the walk in the right direction or toward your desired destination if you do not plan the overall walk one step at a time.

Something as basic as planning for ourselves is usually ignored or put on a secondary list of things to do when there is time. (Some of us don't even plan for next year and heaven forbid asking one of us about five years from now.) But for goals in life to be meaningful, they have to represent personal desires and interests.

It is natural for us to look to other people for ideas or role models; however, we must avoid letting other people dictate the direction we want to go and the road we want to travel. If there is ever a time in your life to be selfish, it is when you are planning your personal goals. Be selfish, be bold, be daring; have it your way. Use the following steppingstones to help you develop your goals.

1. Put It in Print. You don't have no "mojo hand"—magic wand—so write down your goal. Where do you want to go in life? This goal should be comfortable for you; if it is not, then it will be too heavy or cumbersome for you to accomplish. The reason you are writing down the goal is because you will need to see it often. It will also help remind you of why you are doing this in the first place. You need to be able to see where you are going.

When you see your goal written down on paper, it should make you feel good. If you feel good about this goal from the very beginning, you will feel good about accomplishing it. That is why you have to discard the idea that you have a mojo hand. By now you know there is nothing magical about being in control of your life. You have to want it to get it.

Putting your ideas and plans in writing helps you remain focused on your walk. I believe in a certain amount of fate and faith; however, short of having some type of divine intervention and truly possessing a mojo hand, you must take complete charge of your own destiny. Write down your plans and review them daily.

When you are confident that you are ready to set your goals, let other people who share your vision know what you plan to do, not for the purpose of seeking approval but to inform them that you are on your way and headed in a particular direction. You have to examine your goals to see if you are focusing on a specific outcome rather than a process. In other words, make sure that you are not simply going through the motions or what some might call "going around in circles." Looking for a specific outcome will keep you from getting bogged down. As you walk, you will experience a few small successes along the way that will lead you to your final destination.

Think about ends rather than means. After writing down your goals, you will be focused on the outcome rather than the means to get there.

2. Get Out Your Yardstick. The next step toward getting ready to walk the rainbow is writing down the evidence you will accept to prove that you have reached your goal. Some of us have to have proof or evidence that we are making progress. By now I know some of you are saying that this is too much writing. But stay with me a little longer. Let me demonstrate what I mean here. For example, if your goal is to regain the affection of a loved one, the sign of accomplishment would be the return of your old man. How would you measure how well you have accomplished your goal?

Now is the time to lay your cards on the table. You will be the one who decides on the yardstick to measure your expectations. Think about the answer to these questions. What would your goal look like? In the case of the return of the old man, do you want him to send you flowers once a week? Call you once a day? Lay tender, loving kisses on your lips every time you see him? What will it take for him to demonstrate that he loves you?

Another way to do this is by thinking of someone who already has achieved your goal, someone who, in your mind, is the epitome of what you say you want to be. Your job now is to write down the things that person says and the things he or she does that cause you to equate him or her with the goal you want to accomplish. You need to determine what your sign of success will be. If other people are involved in your goal, it will be necessary to inform them about what you expect from them in order to accomplish your goal.

In this case, seeing is believing. If you are examining the life of another person as your role model for a successful life, be sure you see the signs you are trying to emulate. Ask yourself if what you are seeing is what you really want in your life. It is also important to remember that you are looking at the other person as a model; therefore, it is not necessary for you to try to be exactly like that person (or anyone else for that matter). Ultimately, you will define your own path, and everything you want will be available for you.

Many sisters do not know exactly what it is that they want from life. Consequently, they cannot respond well to the questions about the yardsticks to measure the success of their walk. When I encounter sisters who have this problem, I think if they do not know where they are going, how will they know when and if they have arrived?

When responding to questions about evidence of success, do not box yourself in. Try to keep your goals realistic because when you use hypothetical people or situations, there is a danger that your expectations will fall into the hypothetical arena as well. Real people and real circumstances are more effective because you can see more clearly the direction that you want to go. You will also have real evidence to examine when you are dealing with real situations and people.

Whatever you do, approach the situation from a positive perspective. Do this by writing down the action steps you want to take in your life. This will help you determine the visible progress you want and need to make as you walk the rainbow.

3. Dump Excess Baggage. When you get ready to walk the rainbow, having the right type of baggage is essential. This should be a simple concept to understand because sometimes when sisters pack for a trip there is a tendency to overpack. All too often, clothing that is inappropriate for a particular setting is never used and consequently never leaves the bag. The same is true when we plan for a goal. Just as we should take particular care in selecting appropriate items to pack for a trip, we should take equal or greater care in developing the list of action steps necessary to accomplish our goals. Now is the time for you to sort out your list.

If we use the example of a person who wanted to regain her lover, look at the behavior you would expect from the person. You would expect the person to clearly define what she wanted from the relationship and the qualities she would want in a mate. Once she has determined these things, she can then plan how to go about obtaining what she desires. In the same vein, when setting personal goals, you must be clear about what you want and be able to discard what you don't need or desire.

We have control over many of the things we do, and there are a number of cultural things that we do just out of habit. Because other people around us do these things doesn't mean that we have to follow suit. Remember, little sacrifices can lead to big ones. Stop lying to yourself. Your fairy godmother is resting peacefully in heaven, the Easter bunny has retired, and the tooth fairy is not on her way.

Dumping excess baggage means beginning where you are. Tell yourself the absolute truth about your current situation. There are few places in the world (such as the United States) where people are free to make choices regarding their own destinies. However, we enslave ourselves by our self-debilitating habits, toxic friends, unrewarding jobs, expectations from others, lack of money, hopelessness, powerlessness, demands from family, and self-pity. I know that some sisters have had a difficult time in this society, but nobody told you life would be fair. What is real is that you have to take responsibility for yourself.

Packing for the walk over the rainbow is no simple task. It is a major challenge physically, mentally, and emotionally. For example, I realized that I had to do something about my physical appearance as well as my self-esteem.

For a long time, I convinced myself that I was no better or worse off than most of my friends and associates. If everyone close to me was reaching two hundred pounds, what was I to worry about? You can see the fallacy in that kind of thinking. But even with that irrational logic, in my private world, I always knew the self-deceit I was practicing. Every time I looked in the mirror, the lie stared me in the face. I finally reached the point where I understood the deception and accepted the responsibility to dump that psychological and emotional baggage. When I did this, gradually everything began to fall into place.

It was absolutely necessary for me first to accept the fact that no one was going to wave a magic wand or mojo hand to make my life fulfilling. Even though I had a great job (by most standards), I was not fulfilled as a woman. I wanted and needed more enrichment in my life. One major problem still remaining was watching things happen to me instead of working my life plan to make things happen for me. When you take the walk over the rainbow, be sure that the bag you finally decide to take is properly packed.

4. Get Down to the Nitty-Gritty by Recognizing and Keeping the Right Relationships. Why would anybody in her right mind choose to be around people who dishonor her? Yet many of us have relationships with people who disrespect us and we continue to tolerate them. By tolerating these toxic relationships, we have essentially given people permission to disrespect us.

I know it is hard for us to accept that some of the people we love or believe we love cannot give us, in return, the love we need and want. If we believe that we are worthy individuals, how do we reconcile the fact that we let negative people peel away our self-esteem by their destructive nature and interaction with us?

Historically, many African American women have demonstrated tunnel vision when it comes to their men and children. This usually means putting the needs of others ahead of our own. We have learned these roles well from our ancestors and develop our present relationships within this framework—and so we suffer. We play the familiar game of "my man and my kids—they come first; I'll get by." But do we really get by? I don't think so—not well anyway.

We play the "Without a Man/With a Man" game too seriously. We have been programmed to believe that our life cannot be complete without a man in it. Fortunately, a large number of sisters have learned that this is not true and today live very productive and fulfilling lives with or without a man.

In the African American woman's life, this getting by usually takes the form of getting satisfaction in life from other sources. For example, many become great cooks and often do most of the eating, and so their bodies spread. In other cases, we are so preoccupied with taking care of other folks' business that our men start to spread their love around. Our children become more and more dependent on us, and we continue to encourage the dependency for our own psychological gratification of being needed.

If you are in a dysfunctional relationship you believe still has potential, it is easy to stay even when the handwriting on the wall tells you that the relationship is over and you should get out. Learn when it's time to jump ship. Often it is necessary to do so for your physical, mental, and emotional well-being. You may have to leave behind some basic creature comforts you have grown dependent on over the years.

It is easy to assume that the people you love feel the same way you do, but sometimes they do not. In many instances, the love catering we do is not wanted or needed by the people in our lives. We would be better off doing something for ourselves. Sometimes those loved ones even feel suffocated by all of the doting.

There is a stereotype in the African American community that the African American woman is strong, domineering, and capable of doing it all by herself. This Sapphire image is fueled by the media, African American men, and most importantly, by African American women themselves. Sisters have been taught that they can't expect too much from their men because they have been historically and systematically emasculated by the dominant society. A sister cannot be too hard on her children because they are growing up black and facing all kinds of social challenges. She doesn't have much sympathy or empathy left to place upon herself because she has given all of her emotions to everyone and everything else. This does not work. All this does is cripple everybody. The result is we end up living painful lies.

By changing your script and walking the rainbow, you and everyone else will be able to breathe easier. No matter what your past or present thoughts and no matter the level of self-esteem, no one has the right to dump his or her problems on you. There are laws against polluting the environment with toxic waste, so why can't we establish our own personal law against others dumping their toxicity on us? When establishing your law, be sensitive to the needs of others, but do not let their needs dictate yours.

The approval of others is not an essential precondition for believing in yourself. When you have eliminated the need for external approval, you will have the energy necessary to work at reaching your own goals. Recognize your strengths and weaknesses. Listen to people with your head as well as your heart and respond to them accordingly. Distinguish between self-esteem and egotism. Did you know that truly secure people are humble? It is unnecessary to boast about your self-esteem. If you have it, people will be aware of it. It is better to broadcast positive, loving images about yourself by your behavior and watch how positive and loving others will respond.

5. Become a Tagger and Leave Your Mark by Walking Your Talk. Like the tagger who leaves her mark on lintel and post, everyone seems to notice the sister who enters the room poised and confident. We immediately think this is a woman who has control over her life. She appears to us to demonstrate the confidence that shapes her destiny. You may not know where she is headed, but she certainly looks like she knows where she's going. Many of us sisters of the '90s spend so much time forecasting what we are fixing to do that we rarely fix anything. This is a lot like crying wolf. The downside of these false starts is that if you forecast too often but never start or complete anything, when you finally get around to doing something, no one will be paying attention. This could mean that a lot of quality experiences will pass you by before you get tired of waiting to exhale.

What you believe and eventually do will determine the results you get out of life. Therefore, it is absolutely essential that you have the *right* attitude so you can develop the relationships and take the actions that will move you in the right direction and enable you to make your mark on life. Basically, what this means is that you have to move forward with your ideas about what you want from life.

Determine your values and establish your personal integrity, which becomes your mark. People will know what you stand for and will interact with you accordingly. If you must talk about what you want to do in your life, align yourself with the message you are sending so that people around you will see some consistency between your talk and your walk. And be mindful of the fact that everything in life has a price tag and you have to ask yourself if you are willing to pay the price for what you say you want.

The price you pay is consistent with how hard you work for your goals. Practice using personal empowerment, which is usually the tool needed to reach your own goals. Some people call it paying your dues.

The walk over the rainbow, or the quest for personal fulfillment, requires careful attention to the path you want to take in life. Stay on course with your goals and do not wander. By reading this book, you are taking the first step toward achieving your personal fulfillment. Tell yourself—no, declare to yourself—that you will not look back and that you certainly will not let anyone or any circumstance turn you around.

We do not live in isolation from other people. Family members, friends, or others in your life may need to participate in a certain way for you to fulfill your goals. Share your desires and frustrations with supportive people in your life, but do not let other people's opinions control the direction you take.

Did you know that everything we experience in life is about the choices we make on a daily basis? When you establish your personal integrity, you make the choice to maintain control of your life.

Chapter 4

Walking the Rainbow

Beware! Avoid Crabism

By this time some readers may feel saturated by the concept of walking the rainbow and conclude that it is a bunch of hype. Self-confrontation! Self-acceptance! Control over your life! Self-determination! Call it whatever you want. Personal empowerment, with whatever changes it may require, is the most effective way to achieve personal fulfillment, and I believe walking the rainbow is a personal empowerment process.

There was a time in the African American community when the single parent and even two-parent families could depend on their extended family for support. It was not uncommon for two generations to live in the same household. This additional support provided psychological and economic support for the family and the black community. The women in the family had other women within the household to lean on—others who understood their day-to-day trials and tribulations. Today we find ourselves hundreds and thousands of miles away from our support systems, and we have few people whom we view as trustworthy enough for us to share our innermost concerns.

The result of this situation is that we sometimes become bitter and take on attitudes and behaviors that drive us away from each other. We also find ourselves withdrawing from society and falling victim to the "poor-me" blues. It is very difficult and sometimes virtually impossible for some of us to recover from the blues. We get it in our heads that everyone and every set of circumstances are against us. Since we believe this to be true, we adapt our behaviors accordingly. Sometimes we even become the negative person others think us to be and we become vulnerable to "crabism."

Crabism is an old expression in the African American community. It suggests that black folks are like crabs in a barrel. When one of the crabs gets to the top, the crabs on the bottom pull her back down. I never truly understood this concept. I know only that the subject invariably comes up among African Americans when we gather. Nowadays we get embarrassed to admit that we see each other this way. Very seldom will we ever admit that we have these thoughts in mixed crowds. In a way, I'm breaking the code by discussing it here.

African American women have historically focused on nurturing and caring for each other. Yet when we focus on the African American culture as a whole, we see nurturing as an unbecoming characteristic. When you see yourself becoming pessimistic toward life or victimized by the crabism syndrome, you must find a way to break away. Rid yourself of people who are unsupportive of your goals. Keep in mind that you can't help yourself move forward if you are being pulled backward by a pack of backward moving and thinking people.

I have heard numerous testimonies from sisters about how they had just started to make progress when family members and friends appeared on the scene and tried to hold them back. The negativity from these family members or friends distracted them from their goals.

> That was the case with Elaine Bayler, a young woman in northern California whose dream was to become a teacher. She had excellent clerical skills and an outgoing personality. The family and friends who had the most influence on her believed that she would make an excellent secretary. They also believed that she would be able to contribute financially to the family if she pursued this type of work. Every attempt that Elaine made to go back to school to get a teaching cre-

> dential was ridiculed and discouraged to the point where she believed that achieving her dream to be a teacher was impossible. After a while, she believed that she did not have the skills to become a teacher. Yet when she stopped listening to the crabs and developed relationships with people who shared her original vision of herself, she was able to pursue her goals and eventually did become a teacher. Today, she holds a doctoral degree and is a high-ranking school administrator.

Eventually, Elaine refused to let the crabs pull her down. When she listened to the doubts of others, she was not fulfilling her dreams. So be extra careful not to wander too close to the edge while you are walking the rainbow. You have to become such a skillful walker that you do not take an unnecessary tumble. It is important that you listen to the little voice within yourself so that you do not fall victim to crabism. What my parents called crabism, I call dancing on the edge.

You are dancing on the edge when you have finally made up your mind to do something with your life and begin to have doubts that are exploited and magnified by the criticism and lack of support from others around you. Remind yourself that you are now in charge of your life and that you are now walking the rainbow. Affirm to yourself that you will not regress just because someone else does not share your vision.

Keep On Walking

The walk over the rainbow is an individual effort. It cannot be done collectively. Each one of us decides when it is time to take charge of our life. The decision to take charge of your life and begin the walk has to come from you—the person doing the walking. Doubts about what to do or when to take charge pop up all the time. The determined sister learns to acknowledge the doubts, deal with them, and keep on walking her rainbow.

Sometimes when you are trying to achieve your goals, you may experience disappointment and get discouraged. I refer to this as the "last-mile blues," which usually hit when you are the most vulnerable. This disappointment or frustration may cause you to question the direction you are trying to take with your life.

I know that what I'm asking you to do involves intellectual understanding and emotional conviction that you are doing what you truly want to do for yourself. In other words, you can't be half-stepping. By now you should know and believe that nothing can keep you from achieving what you want from life. If you remain faithful to the goals that started you on your self-directed course, along the way you will see large and small signs of growth. Let these signs be your inspiration to keep moving.

There may come a time in your life when you need help or support from others. Do not be reluctant to ask family and friends for help if you need it. Perhaps somewhere in your past you did a favor for other people. Remember how good it made you feel to lend someone else a helping hand? Do not deny others this feeling by refusing to ask for help when you need it. If you perceive asking for support as a weakness, learn a different paradigm. Be strong enough to know when your cause can be assisted by the support of others.

Be Flexible

A few steps out on the walk, you may regress to some of your old debilitating habits. This regression usually takes the form of growth-retarding questions, such as, Is this new action or attitude a big mistake? Has anything come of my efforts or should I even try that activity again? When these questions surface, and they truly will, remind yourself that it takes time to grow.

It takes time to unleash your personal declaration of independence and power. Independence and power do not come instantaneously—they develop gradually in proportion to your efforts. The fulfillment for you is worth the wait. You have to know deep down in your heart that what you have decided you want in your life is right for you.

> On one of my visits to Washington, D.C., I met a woman named Alice Ross who wanted to become a vice president of the company where she was working. Initially she deliberately took a low-paying position in order to get employed with the company. According to this sister, very few African Americans were fortunate enough to gain employment with this prestigious company, and none had ever reached the executive level. Her goal was to become the first African American to do so. Since she was not able to earn the income she wanted and needed at her company, she also worked part-time in the graduate school of business at a local university. This employment situation went on for several years. Although she obtained a slight promotion at the company, she never reached the executive level. At the university, her expertise was relied upon heavily by university officials who were interested in expanding the program in which she was teaching. She eventually left the company with the glass ceiling and is now the first African American to head up a major academic department within the university where she was teaching. Now she sits on the corporate board of the company where she used to work, giving them scholarly advice on how to be a productive enterprise.

Take a lesson from the sister described above: don't think that you have to be rigid with your plans. You may have to make some adjustments at different points along the way. Whatever the case, it is important that you remain focused on your path and remember that no person is wise enough to know just what and how everything should take place. Your job is to use your best judgment to stay focused on your path so that you experience the desired results.

Build Upon Past Experiences

Taking control of and shaping your life means that you will actually go through a psychological and behavioral metamorphosis. The changes you experience when you take control of your life are exhilarating. You will feel empowered to make the critical decisions that chart your course in life. You will know that you can change the things in your life that are not working in your best interest. When you feel this sense of empowerment, you can develop a mental picture of yourself that is consistent with your goals and remain focused on that picture until your behavior completely aligns itself with the image in your mind. If you learn to see problems as camouflaged opportunities, you will surely learn something from each situation you encounter in life. Use the knowledge gained from past experiences to help guide you in the right direction for the future.

When you take control of your life, others around you will know it. Everyone will view your progress toward a new life, which is much like planting a crop. Like a farmer new to farming, you start off with a small crop. Since you are just starting to take greater levels of responsibility for yourself, you start with one small step at a time, taking care to gain something each step along the way. Gradually, you take more and longer steps toward your goal. Like the farmer, you pay close attention to your crop with every expectation for an outstanding harvest—reaching your goals.

Write the Script for Your Life

There is enough evidence to support the idea that each challenge we face in life becomes a teacher in one form or another. What we learn from these challenges propels us through the rest of our lives.

A successful walk over the rainbow depends on you—what you have learned in the past and what you are willing to learn in the future. There will be times when you will feel as if you are between a rock and a hard place. You will get discouraged, but you will not give up because you will know clearly and precisely what it is that you want from life and what you must do to obtain it.

One of the reasons some sisters do not accomplish what they want in their lives is that they are not aware of the cause-and-effect connection between the scripts they allow others to write for them and their own personal lifetime aspirations.

We start at a very early age accepting scripts from other people. These scripts tell us how we should behave, and almost without question, we follow the script. Critics may say that men and women from every culture have life scripts. I am not arguing that point. The point I wish to stress is that the African American woman gets a double dose, which sometimes puts her between a rock and a hard place. She receives one script from the African American community and still another script from mainstream society. This situation is even more complex because the sister also gets a message from the history of the culture that serves as an albatross around her neck. These messages sometimes conflict with each other, often dramatically, and may place the African American woman in a precarious position in her personal and public life. It is clear to me that neither mainstream society nor the African American community will alleviate the stress for the sister. However unfair, this is the environment in which we find ourselves, and we must all decide for ourselves how we will use the messages we receive.

I have come to believe that it is indeed a rare sister who really appreciates her true beauty as an African American woman. How many women do you know who will pull off their clothes, stand before a mirror, and declare, "I am one beautiful sister—I feel like Nefertiti or Cleopatra." It is more likely to be a declaration like this, "I am a mess—what am I going to do with this hair?" I have personally witnessed many sisters bemoaning that some parts of their bodies are too big, some parts too little or in the wrong place, etc.

The media's projection of sisters, for the most part, has not been kind. It reflects something totally different from what we are, and many of us let it cause us too much anxiety. Some of us experience tremendous problems dealing with these contradictions. A good example of this is a sister and her hair. From a very early age, many of us are preoccupied with our hair. This aspect of our life receives very little attention from others, yet it is one of our greatest concerns. In fact, the care of a black woman's hair is easily one of the most lucrative black businesses in America.

The care of a sister's hair can be painful and expensive—the chemicals, the braids, the blow-drys, and of course the marathon waiting that takes place almost every time you visit a salon. Sometimes I wonder if we are being charged for the actual work being done on our hair or rent for the number of hours spent in the salon's space waiting for the stylist to start working. It doesn't matter whether you have an appointment or not—you have to wait. As hard as you may try, seldom do you find a stylist that will make you feel that the wait was worth it. Too often, when we leave, we feel only "acceptable," and in many cases we feel that we could have done the job ourselves at home.

> Nadine, a sister I know in San Francisco, placed such an emphasis on her hair that she purchased an assortment of wigs

> in addition to making weekly visits to an overpriced salon. She was obsessed with her hair. Once she told me that for all the pain she went through, few people ever complimented her on her hair. When she could get anyone to listen, she frequently told stories about how as a young girl, her mother brushed her hair every night hoping that the hair would grow straight and long and shiny. Of course the hair remained kinky, and the sister developed an unhealthy attitude about her appearance—no matter how hard she tried, she was never satisfied with her appearance. From her perspective, she never measured up to the image she was trying to match—the one projected by the media. When this sister eliminated the distorted image from her mind and defined her own appearance, she became a more content person. Today she stills frequents the same expensive salon in San Francisco, but what she walks out wearing is a perfect, natural hair style. Now she tells stories about how strangers stop her on the street, marveled by the natural beauty of her shiny Afro haircut. She feels good because she finally decided to define her own image.

We must learn how to be advocates for ourselves. In other words, we must become aware of the difference between writing our own personal life scripts and allowing others to write scripts for us. It goes back to putting *self* among the top priorities in our lives.

Cast Yourself as the Star

Every day you have to make the choice of how you will live the rest of your life. Why not live life to the fullest? What if you viewed life as a movie? What if you wrote your life script and cast yourself as the star instead of the supporting character? (Remember, the director makes sure that the spotlights are always shining on the star.)

Writing your personal life script and casting yourself in the starring role require you to become and remain aware of those factors in your life that cause you problems. This awareness also makes it possible for you to learn what is wrong on your path over the rainbow and to change course when necessary.

When you decide to cast yourself as the star, there will be dramatic changes in almost every aspect of your life. There will be a change in facial expression, vocabulary, posture, and body language. Your face will project a new kind of radiance. People will notice it right away.

I bet you know sisters who carry themselves as if they were stars. Once you get past your little green monster (read this as crab), you may even admire the way this person thinks so highly of herself. I know I do when I encounter a sister who carries herself in this manner. I appreciate the display of self-confidence that the "sister star" demonstrates.

When you cast yourself as a star, you will immediately notice a change in the way people treat you. One of the major positive attributes of the star is her ability to express herself. Her feelings are worn on her face. When you are cast as the star, even your vocabulary changes. This is very noticeable by others. You will use empowerment words such as I can, I will, I am—words that motivate you to act for yourself, that propel you to the forefront, that match your attitude and make you feel powerful.

Let's face it; sisters inherited the legacy of being advocates for worthy causes. Look at Sojourner Truth, Harriet Tubman, and others. Every cause worth mentioning has a sister somewhere in the picture. If she can serve as such a strong advocate for everyone and his brother, why can't she put some of that energy to work for herself? Even professional football teams have cheerleaders yelling for them. Why can't you? You may be pleasantly surprised when you experience how much better you feel when you start cheering for yourself as well. As negative exterior and internal stresses are reduced, you will experience relaxation and excitement about your life.

When I started to cast myself as the star, I was able to identify and remove roadblocks that prevented me from being my best. You can do it too. Take a tip from how the leading lady acts in the movies. She feels that since the movie is built around her performance, she can tell the director when a particular scene is not right for her.

You are the star and the director. When something in your life is not right for you, acknowledge it and change it. Since you are in charge of the entire script, you decide how you want the movie to end—with you accomplishing your goals.

Very early in life, we make conclusions about ourselves; for example, we subordinate to others. This conclusion is derived from the fact that traditionally, African American women have assumed a subordinate role to our men, our children, and to a large extent, our families and our communities. We wait until others' needs are met before we do much for ourselves. Unfortunately, this conclusion is the first in a series of debilitating conclusions that we draw and impose on ourselves. It is also the faulty foundation that undergirds the distorted image of the African American woman that we struggle with today. It is time for sisters to destroy this faulty foundation so that we can redefine ourselves and correct our distorted identity.

Earlier I mentioned the need to transform from Aunt Jemima to ain't your mama. This means that you will have to take the time right now to rid yourself of any title or label that is unsatisfactory to you. There is no need to put off redefinition of self to some time in the distant future. The present is the perfect time because it is the only time available to you.

Why not redefine yourself today? Use only the best vocabulary when describing what you want for yourself. For example, get comfortable using positive phrases such as

I am an outstanding counselor, I look great in my red silk suit, I do a great job handling complex issues, my work on that last project was superb, I am a great mother, friend, partner, etc. If you make a habit of describing yourself in these terms, others will also get the idea.

Develop a Mental Battle Plan

Over the years, I have observed that African American women seem to have a difficult time communicating their true feelings. By their attitudes they seem to be expressing a great deal of anxiety about their identities. Often one perspective is communicated in public and another in private.

When I talk with sisters in private, they tell me that they are sick and tired of being everything to everybody. They are tired of raising their sons, husbands, and boyfriends. Sisters tell me that, while they enjoy having careers, they would like to have one good brother in the house taking care of business.

I belong to several prestigious black women's organizations and attend large regional and national conferences associated with these organizations. When sisters gather at these events, it is not uncommon for us to sit around talking in small groups. This is when the truth really comes out about our lives.

Sisters say they want the opportunity to be successful in all aspects of their lives without having to give up their careers, aspirations, or meaningful relationships with brothers. If they are not in a relationship, they remain hopeful that in the future they will be in the path of "Mr. Right."

In public, African American women may say that they are happy, if not content, with their present situations. In private, however, they will tell the truth and confess that they are tired of sharing brothers with several other women. They are tired of spending holidays and weekends alone. These women will tell you that they are tired of yo-yo diets, yo-yo dates, and yo-yo child rearing. They will tell you that they are tired of belonging to parasitic black organizations that have lost direction and have purposes even black folks can't relate to. African American women will tell each other that they are tired of explaining why they have begun to date out of the race, while brothers stopped explaining years ago. They will tell you that they are just plain, old-fashioned tired of being tired—tired of waiting to exhale. They want to relax.

Sisters want to be able to not worry about whether the roof will cave in if they do relax. These women will tell you that they want the freedom to be themselves. They no longer want to be held hostage to historical stereotypes or contemporary expectations.

Even though many women will tell you that they believe most problems can be solved if men would just sit down and talk with them, this is highly unlikely because many of us do not yet have the mind-set to really communicate how we feel.

Let me explain what I mean. I refer to communication because effective communication requires an honest exchange of feelings and ideas. It is a two-way process. Many females operate from a feeling of inferiority and find it difficult to participate in an honest dialogue. Before you tell me I'm out to lunch, let me finish with my explanation.

In casting yourself as a star, I asked you to understand that the role of the star requires a different approach than what you may be accustomed to. It requires you to establish a plan of action from a different point of view—a top down instead of a bottom up approach. You must discard the inferior perspective and level the playing field so that you can develop a mental battle plan to accomplish your goals. This approach will definitely require you to change a few things within yourself. It will also require you to help others around you to help them gain a good understanding of what you are about as a person.

Use your mental battle plan as a blueprint for actualizing your life script. When people see that you are serious about changing your position in life, they will be forced to change how they interact with you. By keeping your mind on your mental battle plan, you have actually armed yourself with a personal life-support system. You no longer need to be connected to artificial relationships or false promises. You will then have your own way of accomplishing your goals.

With your mental battle plan in place, your approach is to promote yourself. Remaining consistent with the movie analogy, I am now asking you to assume the role of agent as well. You inform others about your goals and aspirations. In the past you may have been content with people not knowing where you stood or where you were going. Not anymore. As your own agent, your number one goal is to get the best part and deal for your client. Since you are now the director, star, and agent, you get the ultimate satisfaction. You walk away with the agent's commission, the star's salary, and the director's sense of accomplishment. That is a pretty good deal for anyone.

A word of caution. This approach may not work for some sisters because they refuse to take the medicine that will cure them of a crippling disease—"everything to everybody." There is a big problem with this disease. It is counterproductive to the star, and it blocks the implementation of a personal mental battle plan.

Do not let your message get lost. It is important for you to identify your aspirations and consistently communicate them to people in your world. This is not bragging. It reveals your blueprint for success and enables you to attract positive reinforcement.

It is not easy to initiate a mental battle plan of action. If it were, everyone would do it. But you know for yourself that nothing in life worth having comes easily. Many sisters tell me that they have a plan for their lives. But where is the plan and when will it start? Sometimes undeveloped pieces of it are on a crumpled-up napkin that she stuck in her handbag on New Year's Eve. So much for that New Year's resolution.

In some cases, the plan was formulated in the sister's mind, and she even had good intentions of implementing it. But she never got around to fleshing it out so that it became real, so that she would have something concrete to review on a regular basis. Examine the following list for a few suggestions about how to develop a mental battle plan.

1. If you have the habit of putting yourself down, stop doing it and replace the behavior with acknowledging positive things about yourself.
2. Know what you want. Write it down and review your list regularly.
3. Evaluate what you are getting from life. If you are not getting what you want or feel you deserve, change what you are doing and move in the direction where you can get what you want.
4. Visualize what is good for you and associate with supportive people. Go frequently to where you will get the reinforcement you desire and need.
5. Engage in activities that make you feel good. Stop doing the things that bring you down.

An effective mental battle plan for your life will have to be put in writing and reviewed regularly. This is essential. A regular review of your goals along with your battle plan will help keep you focused and conscious of what you are doing or should be doing to accomplish them. You become your own enforcer; no one else will be monitoring your actions to see if you are moving in the right direction. A list of goals on paper is just a useless piece of paper if no action is taken to accomplish them. When you decide to act upon the goals on a regular basis, the goals will soon become your reality.

Be Creative

Walking the rainbow to success, or the quest for personal fulfillment, is a big and complex undertaking. It is also hard work. You have to determine what works for you. The truth is that you must establish goals that ignite a burning passion within you.

Be creative; no one has a monopoly on ideas. Remember what Ralph Waldo Emerson said, "Hitch your wagon to a star." There are a number of places to find stars to hitch on to. The best place to start is with yourself.

For example, when I went to the gym three times in one week, I would treat myself to something nice. Not food, the way I used to, but to a nice facial or pedicure. I got really carried away once and bought myself a round-trip ticket to Las Vegas. So that it would really seem like a gift, I had the travel agent send it to me in the mail instead of me picking it up like I used to. The travel agent participated in my game; the cover letter from the agent congratulated me on being a good girl. Believe me, I appreciated that letter when I got it because it was a visible way of reinforcing my value and it had come from within me.

Be truly creative; make a list of things that get you excited and see how creative you can be in using this information to accomplish your goals. Examine the following areas of your life: your social and spiritual life, your body, your skills and talents, your intelligence, and your ability to create money.

When was the last time you conducted a personal asset inventory? What are your major assets? Make a list of your strong points and decide how you can use them. These strong points should be ready to wear, not things that will take a lot of ironing out while you are walking over the rainbow. If we were really talking about clothes, I would say take clothes that are wrinkle-free (your good stuff). On this list do not include things you hope to have or things you have on layaway at your mental department store. Remain focused on what you know you have that you can readily pull out of the bag and use immediately.

You will also need to make a list of your liabilities. This list is very important because it will be a part of the baggage you will want to leave behind as you depart for your trip over the rainbow. If you have some liabilities that you know about and can't get rid of before you start your trip, keep your eye on them, but as you get stronger, discard them on your walk. Your goal is to reach the end of your journey with few or no liabilities.

When all is said and done, you have to have faith in yourself—it is the key to initiating and achieving your goals. Faith in yourself will make the difference between starting your walk and finishing your walk.

We have already concluded that the star owns the spotlight. We also know that in order to remain the star and in the spotlight you have to perform, and you have to be creative. In Hollywood, only the most creative scripts and most accomplished actresses get the Oscar. In real life, only those people with specific scripts for their lives successfully accomplish their goals.

Chapter 5

Reaching and Living at the End of the Rainbow

Maintain a Positive Self-Image and Outlook

One of the hardest things for me to do when I was walking my rainbow was to visualize myself as successful. Sometimes, it was not easy to see myself as successful even though others thought me to be.

For a number of years, I did not take ownership of my personal and professional success. The mind-set that I was a sharecropper's daughter so overwhelmed my vision that I could not see beyond my humble beginning. I could not even accept my accomplishments. To me, success was temporary. From this perspective, I could see myself back in the fields of rural east Texas doing hard labor. My paradigm of myself was still stuck in the past. My mind refused to let my self-image and self-esteem move forward with my real-world gains.

There were times when juxtaposing my frozen mental image of my past world and my present-day existence caused unbearable pain. I was caught between two worlds: one that told me that I was a successful college administrator and the other that reminded me that the escape from the world I left behind might only be temporary if I made the wrong move. My intent here is not to revisit the psychosocial history of African Americans in the United States but rather to point out the impact of the dynamics of that history on my psychological security as an adult.

Unfortunately, I learned to develop negative feelings about my color and my sex. Fortunately, I was able to unlearn these cultural contaminations without much permanent damage to my psyche. In order to do so I had to find a way to live a balanced life that put into proper perspective my humble beginnings as well as the race and gender challenges confronting me. Using my personal empowerment approach of walking the rainbow, I rescued my psyche. I was able to wrench myself free of self-imposed problems and confront external ones as they materialized. I took my life into my own hands. You can too. The next step for me was to sustain this empowerment at the end of the rainbow.

Establish a Balanced Lifestyle

At the end of the rainbow you will have reached your goals. But how do you maintain them? Sustaining a balanced lifestyle requires daily reinforcement. For example, develop a positive outlook, learn personal confidence, expand your thinking, and develop new ways to live a balanced life.

How great do you want to be? It is within your power to define your own image of greatness. If you find yourself in two worlds, you can change by adjusting your attitude. The competing and challenging worlds of "victimization" ("I can't") and "empowerment" ("I will") become a necessary part of your lifestyle. You learn to freely exchange these in your daily vocabulary. This does not have to be difficult for you, but it can cause creative tension. Why work hard all your life to accomplish goals if you do not enjoy the results of the hard work? Do not become one of the statistics—the people who worked hard just to retire and never lived to enjoy the retirement.

Work actively to broaden your horizons; the more areas you can be a part of, the more valuable you and your ideas will become. Learn to transcend the old self. By establishing balance in your life, you can establish joyous connections with others. Everyone needs balance in his or her life. Most successful people seem to have a healthy balance between work and play.

At the end of the rainbow, unite from the head and the heart. Explore your own greatness and potential. You have accomplished your goals—you have earned the right to feel like the positive person you always aspired to be. You have learned the million-dollar secret! Accept into your heart only those people and those ideas and suggestions that ring true, and let go of those that do not.

At the end of the rainbow, there may be a number of people in your life now who will not be able to stand the weather because you will be just too hot to handle.

Now that you are focused and have walked the rainbow, you must define your personal peace, which comes from your inner world. Recall the cause-and-effect principle: You create what you experience and you experience what you create.

Your great challenge is not to be distracted by what comes in front of you, pulls on you, or calls to you. Your goal and challenge will be to remain focused on your own script—the one you developed, wrote, and implemented for yourself.

Tension is created when you challenge yourself to transcend external obstacles. It is released when you take control over your life and establish greater and more fulfilling challenges for yourself.

Personal fulfillment empowers you to display self-confidence and live according to your own desires. It is important to remember that your attitude remains the gateway to the new life you have constructed and the person you have chosen to become.

Establish Strategies for Managing Problems

By the time you reach the end of your walk, you will have had time to practice being yourself. Know how to value yourself and your time. Sisters who do not remain focused on their own lives and personal selves will continue to experience frustration and disappointment in life. So do not be pulled into inner power struggles with yourself. The personal conflicts about the direction you should take in life have disappeared because you have changed the way you think. You have been willing to let go of a limited perspective and have enlarged the way you view yourself.

Some lessons in life will be more painful than others. One of the lessons that was the hardest for me to grasp and adhere to was that I had to walk away from toxic people. Toxic people are persons who view whatever you do as not good enough.

As a result of my walk over the rainbow, I discovered the importance of leaving toxic parasites behind. Doing this was vital in order for me to remain focused. In order to save myself, I had to free myself from people who were detrimental to my balance. This will be especially difficult for women who feel they are everything to everybody, who feel that if they let go for even a brief time that things will fall apart.

A sister who tries to please everybody ends up being nobody herself. You cannot leave something until you love it. The more you hate something, the more bound you are to it. The more you love something or someone, the freer all involved become.

Living at the end of the rainbow, you live and let live. Like some of you, I had to learn that when love is truly meaningful, it is not physically binding. Loved ones are free to come and go at will. At the end of the rainbow, you understand all of this because you have a balanced life.

You understand the freedom and empowerment that come with loving and being loved. Everyone has a part to play in establishing and maintaining the parameters of the relationships in their lives.

Living at the end of the rainbow means that you are no longer enslaved by your past. You will realize that, positive or negative, everything in your past happened for your own good. Closely examine this statement. It took me a long time to understand that the mind is not capable of leaving the past behind. It stores up everything, negative and positive.

To preserve a positive state of mind, you have to maintain a clear psychological reservoir. Release things that do not fit your new image or lifestyle.

Sustaining a productive life at the end of the rainbow will require you to find ways to manage your emotional behavior. So don't buy into the myth "It is in a sister's nature to express her feelings in a 'Sapphire' manner." This image portrays her as someone who can't control the way she feels. Falling for this myth is a cop-out. At the end of the rainbow, you know that the Sapphire image is really bottled up self-depreciation.

Many of the sisters who play the Sapphire game rarely, if ever, get to the core of their true emotional concerns. The recipient of Sapphire's wrath is so busy dealing with her behavior that her message or point is missed or camouflaged.

Learn to take personal responsibility for how you feel about the way people treat you. This is not easy to do, but at the end of the rainbow, it is imperative. When you start to take responsibility for expressing yourself without building up anger and resentment, you feel good. It really is a personal choice; you can choose to feel good and still tell it like it is.

Destroy the Stereotype of Colored People's Time (CPT)

In chapter 1, I asked you to confront yourself and look at your attitude. Now it is time for you to take a close look at how you use your time. If you are really sincere about living productively, you cannot ignore how you use your time. Do you really value your time, or do you just give it away without thinking about it?

At the end of the rainbow, you must know how to manage your time. You also must know that CPT is not a valid time management practice. CPT (the habit of showing up late for meetings or appointments) is a stereotype that is not productive because it tells others that you are not dependable and suggests that you do not value the time of others.

You must take charge of your time and guard it carefully; it is and will always be one of your most valuable possessions.

Each person gets a twenty-four-hour allocation of time each day. If your plan for using your time is different from what you actually do, how much is it costing you in productivity? Do you even care or pay attention to how you use your time? Get rid of the term "spare time." At the end of the rainbow, you do not have any spare time.

The phrase "use it or lose it" is a most appropriate description of how we should manage our time. The misuse of time is one of the major reasons for a lack of progress toward one's goals. The misuse of your time could prevent you from achieving something very valuable—your dreams.

Misuse of your time can also prevent you from living life to the fullest. At the end of the rainbow, it is a good idea to refrain from activities that waste your time. Use your time to your advantage. When I finally sat down and analyzed how I was using my time, I was very surprised at not only how much time I wasted but also how I allowed other people to waste my time.

Your time is by far one of your greatest resources. Before I learned how to use my time effectively, it was also a big obstacle and trap. Without knowing it, I was going through life wasting valuable time on insignificant activities.

Basically, time is what we use to measure our passage through life and to record that we have been here. Time is probably one of the most sought-after stocks on the market, yet it cannot be purchased on Wall Street. Stockbrokers can invest your money and make you large sums of it, but you are the only one that can invest your time.

While time is your greatest asset and resource, it can also be your greatest liability or curse. You can become highly stressed if you habitually use your time ineffectively or allow others to misuse it.

If you are like some women, you spend a great deal of time doing things for other people. For example, you put your plans for something on the back burner. Sometimes you enjoy this personal sacrifice; you feel like a martyr. When those around you do not acknowledge you for this martyrdom, you feel abused and used. Wouldn't it be more productive from the beginning if, in pursuit of a more productive life, you changed the way you use your time?

If the manner in which you are using your time is different from the way you feel comfortable using it, you will eventually rebel either internally or externally. Probably both. You will become dissatisfied with yourself and with those around you. This dissatisfaction can prevent you from sustaining the gains you made when you walked the rainbow. Ultimately, it will inhibit your lifestyle and prevent you from accomplishing further goals.

Keep a record of how you use your time. This record will help you assess your productivity. Simply put, wasting your time is tantamount to squandering the pot of gold you found at the end of the rainbow. Stay in control of your time and stay in control of your life. I am not talking about using some long, drawn-out time management system where you have to develop ten or twelve charts in order to assess your time. I am talking about a basic principle of recording the use of your time and reviewing your notes regularly.

Bear in mind that you cannot retrieve yesterday and you cannot borrow from tomorrow. In his book *The Seven Spiritual Laws*, Deepak Chopra said, "The past is history, the future is a mystery, and this moment is a gift. That is why this moment is called the present." This very minute is the only time you can spend. Why not make the most of it? Decide now how you will use your next twenty-four-hour allotment.

As African American women, we should understand and appreciate this time management principle. Some of us are quick to refer to ourselves as the double minority because we are African American women. This label sometimes implies that African American women have twice the burden: being a woman and a minority person. Likewise, some of us do not hesitate to recite the various forms of discrimination that may be heaped upon African American women as a result of living in a white male-dominated society.

It is not uncommon to hear sisters recount how they have encountered unfair practices because of their race and gender. We cannot make these allegations about our allotment of time—it is freely given to us without respect to race or gender.

I refer to time as the great equalizer. It discriminates against no one. Every man, woman, and child gets the same fair share—100 percent of every twenty-four hours. The real question is, how much of this valuable resource do you use for yourself?

Managing your time is directly related to the points we covered in the discussions on confronting yourself, planning goals, sticking with your plans, and writing your scripts for life. You are at a crossroads. You are at the point where you have to decide whether time is to be your friend or your enemy.

I decided I wanted time to be my own friend. There were times when I worked so intensely, so productively, for one hour that the output gave the appearance of my having worked for a full day. Then there were days that I got lost in the twenty-four hours and did not work them to my advantage.

Time can be a yardstick for measuring where you are now and where you want to be in the future. From this perspective, controlling your time and your life equals making the right choices at the right time on a day-to-day basis.

Be as Bold as You Wanna Be

There is a kind of price you pay when you reach the end of the rainbow. You will no longer want to have the option to shift responsibility for your life to anyone else. You will gladly assume this responsibility. And, more than likely, everyone's expectations of you will change. You will certainly expect different things of yourself. Depending upon the changes people see in your attitude and the visibility of your accomplishments, individuals will more than likely change their expectations of you. In some cases, friends may wander away from you because you are preoccupied with your own goals. Your task will be to remain focused on your personal goals and make the right choices and select the right alternatives for your life.

Stay away from power struggles with people who have opposing plans for you. Accept a person's point of view as his or her own. You do not have to agree. What you do have to do is stop fighting with yourself and understand that what is happening to you right now is preparing you for something magnificent in the future.

Personal fulfillment means that you have to learn to love yourself. Count the ways in which you love yourself.

How high can you count? Take a "love myself" inventory. Make a list of ten ways or reasons why you love yourself. I would be willing to bet good money that the average sister will have a difficult time coming up with ten.

One of my major pastimes is coaching sisters on how to love themselves first. Even highly trained, successful sisters seem to be expressing lukewarm love for themselves. If you made it over the rainbow without a high dose of self-love, I would be very surprised. But let us say you are a rare one who became successful and got over the rainbow with a low grade of self-love. One thing is certain—you will not be able to remain at the end of the rainbow without upgrading your feelings about yourself.

When I coach sisters on how to love themselves, some are quick to resurrect old excuses as to why they cannot do something different with their lives. Their list of excuses might include I am overweight, I am over the hill, I got grey hair too early, I cannot find Mr. Right, I am too old to start over again, my children still need me, my cash flow is too low, I am too tired, my health ain't what it used to be, I'm going through the change and it has changed my life. When I hear them say things like this, I tell them that this alibiing is not productive and won't work at the end of the rainbow.

The majority of things on the lists are topics that they can do something about any time they are ready. When I examined my excuse list, I got embarrassed about what I saw. I scolded myself for waiting so long to do something about the things that were unsatisfactory to me, e.g., my personal life, my weight, my job, my children. While I could develop a long list of excuses about why my life was not good, I experienced a difficult time coming up with ten reasons for loving myself.

Quite frankly, it is sad now to admit it, but I was able to list only two reasons for loving myself. The two reasons were not even about me—they were about my two children. That was the day I broke down and cried for me. It was also the day I decided that another day would not pass without my figuring out why I could not list some reasons that I loved myself.

If you have trouble listing things you love about yourself the first time around, keep trying. After a while, you will become more comfortable.

To love yourself, you have to accept yourself as you are right now—not tomorrow or next week. I recommend making a contract with yourself. The contract would include the following:

> I hereby agree to love myself, appreciate myself, validate myself, and support my progress, my beliefs, and my values.

Such a contract, if executed and implemented without reserve, will sustain you at the end of the rainbow.

To further sustain myself at the end of the rainbow, I developed the following love-me exercise. I started out by saying affirmations like these: I love my sexy brown eyes; I love my mouth—what a sweet mouth; I love my sense of humor—I like making people laugh; I love myself for being fair, etc. After I got in the habit of doing the self-love affirmations, it started to get a little bit easier (if not marginally egotistical). One day I ended up with three pages of affirmations. Guess what? I loved it.

(Anyway, it was my personal list, and I was not thinking of hanging it over the busiest freeway in town or on my wall at the office.)

Stop Singing Old Songs

As a young girl growing up, I used to listen to my grandmother and some of her friends discuss their lives. While we may truly respect, admire, and love the contributions of our ancestors, we must not compare ourselves to sisters of three or four generations ago. This does not mean that we are better than the sisters who came before us—only that we are living in different times. But in many ways we still have the same agenda.

My intention here is not to resurrect the historical controversy of the black female matriarchy or discuss the dysfunction of black male-female relationships. My sole point here is to say that too many sisters feel guilty about being successful when their brothers are not experiencing a similar degree of success. They feel in some way that their success is keeping the brothers from gaining their rightful place. I say that it is not an either/or situation. Both can exist in a parallel fashion.

To gain maximum benefit from being at the end of the rainbow, a sister has to understand that her life should be the one thing that she can take charge of and control. If she does this successfully, I suspect she will be in great shape to help others and still love every minute of it.

Learn to let go of any guilt you have about yourself or any past behaviors. Guilt will only cloud your vision. Practice affirming your love for yourself on a regular basis. Your life's goals come from the heart. Stay focused and accomplish what you desire in life.

Assert your life's aspirations with compassion and passion at the end of the rainbow. You are no longer at a standstill waiting to exhale. Do not let others' judgment of you block your self-love. Do not let your own negative judgment block your self-love. It has been said that every time you judge yourself or others, you separate yourself from your capacity to see clearly and love unconditionally.

Today is the perfect time for you to place the right value on yourself. You are worth every million.

Don't Wait to Exhale

At the end of the rainbow, remain focused on the present; you cannot relive the past nor can you transport yourself to the future. Therefore, operate from a position of strength—reach out in love. By focusing your attention and love in the present, you send love into the future and release it to the past. The cause and effect of this attitude will have tremendously positive results.

The more you acknowledge and express your appreciation for how much you are receiving from the present, the more positive your expectations can be for the future. You can create whatever you want from life with this attitude. It is your right to feel this way.

Your beliefs and attitude about your world create your experiences in the world. Even after you have completed the walk over the rainbow, you have to take care of the business of living your life to the fullest. I am not going to tell you that you will never have the blues again. But you can use personal empowerment ideas to deal with the blues.

You know as well as I do that talk is cheap. When I launched my so-called honor-thyself or love-thyself campaign, I had some false starts. I came up short a couple of times. It did not take a long time for me to reach the conclusion that the success of my efforts would depend on me. I had to be committed to staying in control of my life.

Live by your values or you will have to change them to match the way you live. Why do I tell you to live by your values? It is the only way to live in harmony with yourself at the end of the rainbow. At the end of the rainbow, you have accomplished your goals. Your behavior should be geared toward maintaining those goals.

To live otherwise would mean that your quest to control your life and destiny would have been in vain. Your values and belief systems are the blueprint by which other people interact with you.

Each of us has the tools to enable us to live our lives at ease at the end of the rainbow. There is no need to act impulsively. All we have to do is choose to use our personal empowerment skills to stay in control of our lives. We all choose when it is time to make our personal evolution.

Discover and enjoy the joy that awaits you at the end of the rainbow. Enjoy your walk over the rainbow. Don't wait to exhale! Do it and do it now.

Chapter 6

The Principles in Action

Sharing with Others

My name is Claudia. I am the personality the author created to tell you the story of how the "right to" or "empowerment" principles can be used and applied to your everyday life.

Throughout the remainder of this chapter, you will be introduced to the principles I used to help me focus on what I wanted to do with my life. This chapter demonstrates how my six friends and I applied the principles covered in this book to achieve our own declarations of independence and fulfillment. On the following pages, you will discover as we did that every day is a new opportunity for you to start your walk over the rainbow. After reading this book, you will never want to participate in another "poor-me" discussion or attend anymore "misery loves company" socials. You will stop waiting to exhale—you will live life to the fullest.

Session One

I was sitting on my couch listening to Julia Smith, one of the girls in our monthly support group, which was formed about a week ago. There are seven members in the group. Our New Year's resolution was to make ourselves over physically and mentally. We decided that we needed a new attitude to go along with the new bodies we were building in the gym every week. It really is interesting the way all of this got started. The seven of us belong to an athletic club.

New Year's Eve, we made a pact to go to the gym three times a week instead of our usual three times a year.

Sometimes after the gym, we would go to a restaurant with the intent of having coffee or tea or just to talk; however, more likely than not, we would eat. Some of us needed no encouragement to stuff ourselves with all types of appetizers. In addition to the tea and coffee, we would have nachos, potato skins, and other equally unhealthy foods.

Last week at one of the talk sessions after our workout, I refused to eat the potato skins. My refusal irritated my friend Julia. "Why aren't you having skins, Claudia?" Julia demanded, almost yelling from across the table.

"I just don't care for any at this time. Eating like this defeats the workout we just had," I responded defensively.

"We deserve to treat ourselves after a workout like the one we just had. Anyway, you know most of us are not going to stick to this routine. I go through this every year and I never finish anything," Julia said, looking sheepish. Now everyone at the table was looking at her with their heads slightly tilted down as if to avoid looking at each other. I sensed that we were all just a little embarrassed because most of us felt pretty much the way Julia did about not finishing things in our lives. We sat there looking at each other in silence for what seemed to be about five minutes. I finally broke the silence.

"Well, that is not going to happen this year." No one said a word. Their eyes told me that I needed to say more. "It will not happen this year because we will be there for each other to keep the reinforcement going. Won't we, ladies?" I asked, having no idea what type of response to expect or where I was actually going with my declaration. Julia was waiting for me like a ferocious lion waiting to attack her prey.

"So, tell us, Miss Infinite Wisdom, what magic wand are you going to wave to transform us? No, let me just say transform me. I must have been born under some kind of jinx or something. It takes me forever to finish anything, and that's after it has taken me forever to get started."

I took the bait. "We will have monthly support group sessions. I'll coordinate. What we have to do is take charge of our lives and determine what we want out of life and do it. We have to stop sitting around holding our breath waiting for somebody or something to do a quick fix for us. We have to do like my grandma used to say back home. We have to get out there and walk that rainbow, girlfriend."

Even before I got that last sentence out of my lips, somehow I knew I was committing myself to a major challenge. How was I going to chart a course for seven women, myself included? I did not have a clue about my next step.

"Show up at my place next Friday night; I'll lay out the plan," I blurted out, trying to be confident and convincing. I don't know whether they believed I had a plan or not. They all agreed to come to my house on Friday for me to unveil the master plan for our transformation.

I decided to take the challenge seriously. I'm a teacher at a university, and I know enough not to go to class unprepared. Every time I create a class, I like to have plenty of time to research the subject. This time I had only one week to develop the plan for my friends and, yes, for myself.

During the next week, at work and after work, I was at the library and the bookstores trying to find material appropriate for our sessions. I looked at self-help, motivational, health and fitness, spiritual, and metaphysical books. Nothing I examined seemed appropriate for our group. By the time Wednesday rolled around, I was almost ready to call it quits. By Thursday, panic set in and I decided to be creative and develop my own material for our group using the right to ideas discussed in this book, *Walk the Rainbow*. These empowerment principles were absolutely ideal for what we were about to undertake.

On Friday night, much to my surprise, they all showed up. Sheila and Barbara were the first to arrive. Both are accountants and work for the same CPA firm. They are married to brothers, and they do almost everything together. Julia had told me that Sheila and Barbara were so close that they decided to get pregnant at the same time. Dorothy, Paula, and Shirley were the next to arrive. The three of them work together at a beauty college. Between the three of them they have over forty years of experience in the beauty business. Julia, my best friend and an attorney, was the last one to show.

When they first arrived, I told them to relax and get comfortable. Our meeting was set for seven o'clock. I only served them hot tea. Sitting in my living room, Julia was the first to speak.

"Before you unfold your master plan for us, Claudia, could you please tell me where is the food? Even college professors make enough money to buy some cheese and crackers," Julia said teasingly but serious as a heart attack.

"No food at these meetings. Eat before you come. Seven o'clock is too late for us to be stuffing ourselves," I said, waiting for protests from the rest. It was a surprise to me that I didn't get static from the rest of the group. They just sat there waiting for me to go on. So I did.

As I explained to the group what we would be doing at our session, it became clear to me that these women were serious, and I was glad that I had taken the time to work out a plan that I believed would be meaningful for all of us.

"Ladies, after thinking about this project of ours, it is evident to me that we will all have to make a commitment to help each other."

They all nodded their heads in agreement. I went on to tell them that to go in the direction we all needed, it was necessary that everyone have faith in our ability to accomplish our goal. We have to give each other support.

"Yea, Claudia, get on with the point—we all went to Sunday school. We know about faith and what it can do for you," Sheila interrupted.

"Yes, but do we all know and accept the fact that giving comes easily for women, that we are brought into this world giving? It is important for all of us to accept and understand that this very concept could be the root cause of some of our problems," I responded.

Everyone was really into the conversation now. I was pleasantly surprised and felt a little more comfortable with the idea of this support group. I have been teaching for over twenty years and feel at ease with a group of energetic and eager graduate students. However, trying to present this program to my friends was an extremely different story altogether.

"Are you saying that I am the reason for feeling the way I do, that I'm the reason I've hit the glass ceiling at my job? I don't think so, darling. You have to come by me again with that logic," Julia challenged.

"No, I'm not saying that exactly."

"Exactly what are you saying then?" Barbara chimed in.

"I'm saying that any personal growth requires us to look at ourselves first. For those of us who are willing to participate in life to the fullest, we will find that there really is no limit to the personal fulfillment we can enjoy because there is no limit to our great inheritance from our creator," I said.

"That sounds like something right out one of those feel-good books—easy said, harder to do," Barbara said half-joking and half-serious.

"I know what you're saying, Barbara. There are times when we feel that other people seem to attract all of the rewards in life. That's why I thought we would start our sessions by getting a good perspective on our own situations in life. Ultimately, we all have to ask ourselves some very basic questions, and we have to personally take responsibility for answering these questions," I said, trying not to sound like I was preaching.

"Do you plan to tell us what these questions are before the night is over?" Paula asked provocatively.

"Yes, ma'am. The first question is, Who are you and how do you see yourself? Another question along the same line of thinking is, Do you know where you're going and do you even know why you want to go there?" I was on a roll. These questions were my platform for the evening. The ladies, with their probing minds, had given me the perfect opening to get us focused. I was relieved.

"Those are some pretty heavy-duty questions," Julia commented.

"I know that. But if we are going to get off the dime, they have to be addressed by each and every one of us. It is important that we see with our own eyes that the answers to these questions, in essence, deal with our own sense of self. These questions make us examine our goals and our assets as well as our liabilities. When we start to examine these questions, we have to look ourselves right in the face," I stated authoritatively, defying Julia to challenge me.

"I agree with Claudia, because if we are not serious enough about this to look at ourselves, we can't move forward. The way I see it, if we do not handle these questions, we're playing games with each other and, more importantly, ourselves," Shirley spoke out, validating what I wanted to do.

I told them that the frustration and stagnation we were experiencing with our lives could be a general reflection of how we see ourselves in relation to each other and the world. We do have to be willing to take the time to look at our face in the mirror.

"I just need to know one thing, ladies. Are we willing to take this first step toward gaining control over our lives?" Everyone nodded yes; they were willing to move forward.

"This is not as hard as it sounds. Let me share this thought with you. Many of us are reluctant to confront or examine ourselves because we are simply afraid of losing the self that we have grown accustomed to," I said in a tone again just short of preaching.

"I am not afraid of losing myself. I just don't know what I would replace myself with at this time in my life. That's the scary part," Julia said, looking painfully honest.

Barbara joined in then. "I can go along with that. I have a tendency to resist any kind of change, and I think I feel that way because it is the comfortable thing for me to do."

We all nodded and confirmed Barbara's concern about why we don't want to change.

"Unfortunately, we usually define ourselves in terms of what we do for other people and not in terms of what we do for ourselves. In most cases, we cannot easily explain why we even do the things we do," I said, moving closer to the edge of the seat.

Almost jumping off her seat, Shirley threw her hands over her head in a move you see at church when the spirit has hit you and you begin to testify. "Amen, I know the feeling, honey. I am so frustrated with that attitude we have. I am sick and tired of being defined and redefined by what I have rather than what I am. Claudia, I don't know about the rest of the group, but I am ready to take this walk. I want to sort out all my mess."

From looking at the faces of the other ladies around the room, I could tell that they were all ready to start the walk over the rainbow. They were already looking at how they could answer those questions. A question from Barbara got me back in focus.

"Claudia, give me some idea about how I can best go about confronting myself realistically. The others might have a handle on this, but I am lost."

"Barbara, there is no best or single way to look at yourself. How we see ourselves is largely dependent upon our awareness of self. It is through this awareness that we express ourselves to the world. Your image of yourself is what you consciously show to the public. What you feel and what you see in the mirror every day are reflections of where you see yourself in relation to other people."

"Are you saying that I compare myself to the rest of you guys? No wonder I am so pitiful," Julia said, cracking up. Everyone else laughed along with her.

Trying to bring some composure back to the group, I said, "Ladies, seriously, in order for us to make progress in this whole issue of self-confrontation, we have to look at our own self-imposed expectations. I'm talking about the aspirations and the expectations you place upon yourself. Believe me, these expectations are linked to your feelings of self-esteem. I say they are linked because they help us establish within ourselves what we label as our successes or our failures." I was about to continue, but Julia interrupted me.

"I am so damn sick and tired of hearing about self-esteem. I may not think I am a superstar, but I sure in the hell don't hate myself either."

Before I could respond, Dorothy, who had been relatively quiet all evening, spoke out very sharply. "Cut the crap, Julia. You are always talking about yourself, putting yourself down. We hear you all the time. I'm too fat. I'm not good at this or that, I wish I could, and so on, and so forth. Why don't you just be quiet for a change and let Claudia finish explaining the lesson?"

I continued with the explanation. "While we are going through our lessons, I would like us to agree that we will be patient with each other and most of all with ourselves. We don't have to refer to those nagging doubts as lack of self-esteem. Some people call them demons. What I'm talking about are those things that bring us down—things that keep us from doing the things we need to do and prevent us from feeling good about ourselves. Of course, it goes without saying that what is viewed as a successful experience for me may be detracting for you. That is exactly why I said we have to address our questions from our own personal perspective."

"What is hard for me to understand is where all this low self-esteem came from in the first place. I didn't always feel this low about myself. I don't even know when it started," Shirley said.

"That is a good observation, Shirley. Our feelings of self-worth or lack of self-worth are developed from the way other folks look at us. Other people's attitudes toward us shape our attitudes about ourselves. In order for us to change how we feel about ourselves, we have to change the way we interact with others," I said.

"Hello, Earth to Paula, Earth to Paula. You guys might think I'm slow or something, but you know, I think I'm just catching on to what Claudia has been saying—that it's important for us to examine ways to preserve and protect ourselves from bad situations. Like that hostile marriage of mine. No wonder I feel like hell most of the time," Paula said, looking like someone who had suddenly discovered a piece of gold.

I used Paula's revelation to tell them that the "self" is our most personal and valued possession. I said, "How we view ourselves will depend on our own personal expectations and what we think society expects of us. The frustration we experience on a daily basis is largely dependent on self-imposed expectations." I challenged them further by telling them that they had to determine realistic expectations and how to accurately interpret those expectations of each other. I told them that their personal self-confrontation would reveal their "true" attitude, physical bodies, and personal level of achievement.

"Hold it just one minute, Claudia. When we first started this discussion, you said that my self-esteem was connected to the rest of you," Julia said, almost yelling.

"Julia, in a nutshell, what I said is that personal understanding and acceptance come from staying focused on who you are on your own terms. It is also important to accept who you are and determine the direction you want to go in life. Once this is in place, you will not have trouble processing why you want to go in the direction you are going,"

I responded defiantly, hoping to avoid a confrontation with my best friend.

"Julia's attitude is her problem. She can't or doesn't want to understand nothing. She is always coming off with the negative trip. I hope she will leave it out of the sessions," Sheila laughed while giving Barbara the high-five sign. "I guess we are a little late for that tonight."

I decided that I needed to seize this opportunity to move to my next point, which was about attitude. We had been going now for about an hour and a half with no break. I told them to take a ten-minute break and get some tea and stretch. I needed the time to figure out how I would get them on the subject of attitude without "pissing" them off. I knew this group pretty well; therefore, I knew this topic would be my biggest challenge for the evening. So far, the approach I was using, asking them questions and getting them to think, was working pretty well. I decided that right after the break, I would start off with a question about attitude.

After the break, Dorothy was the first one to speak. "Claudia, I want to say something about attitude. All of us have an attitude. I got one about how some people seem to enjoy putting each other down. It ain't necessary for me to call no names, 'cause they both know who they are," Dorothy said, looking at Sheila and Barbara as only African American women do when they really want to stress a point.

Watching my friends now, I realized that they were portraying the exact point I wanted to make about attitude. I decided to dive in head first. "Ladies, the way we are coming at each other this very moment is a reflection of our attitude toward each other," I said.

"Yea, let's keep it clean. I can get negative shit at work and I don't care to have it on my own time. Claudia, go ahead and make a point worth listening to, will you?" Julia said in a very authoritative and sarcastic tone.

Sheila had been relatively quiet all evening. Suddenly she came alive and lashed out at Julia, "You are sickening to me. Where do you get off ordering people around all the damn time? Everything has to be on your schedule, on your terms. The only thing more sickening than you is Claudia, who seems perfectly happy letting you rule her."

No one was prepared for Sheila's reaction—least of all me. Everyone was looking at me and I felt trapped into responding. "Sheila, I understand Julia. Her behavior does not bother me in the least," I said, partially telling the truth. I hated to admit it, but Julia's bossiness did get on my nerves sometimes but not enough for me to bring it into the session.

Sheila tried to respond but she was interrupted by Julia. "What does my attitude and my relationship with Claudia have to do with you? You should spend more time checking out your own attitude. It is your 'door-mat' personality that you need to work on."

I interjected. "Julia, you can get your point across without being so ugly about it."

"And you can stop trying to create perfect little worlds and perfect little situations with perfect little people in them because they do not exist," Julia retorted, practically screaming at me.

This situation was not going the way I had expected. I came pretty close to panic but decided to focus on getting my friends to calm down, so I asked, "What color is our attitude now, ladies?"

Paula responded, "Flaming red and getting hotter by the minute." She spoke in such a tone that everybody broke out in laughter. After we regained our composure, I tried to bring some order back to the discussion.

"The way we were behaving toward each other is really a reflection of our state of mind. We have a choice about the way we behave toward each other here in this room and with people outside of this room. Frankly, I do not like the way we just acted toward each other," I said.

"I haven't said much tonight because I wanted to wait and see if we were *truly* real about wanting to do something about our lives. I know I am a miserable person most of the time. In the past, I never gave it much thought. Now, listening to Claudia, I'm wondering if I can turn that around. I believe I would like to do that," Paula said sincerely.

This comment from Paula seemed to be just what we needed because the rest of the evening went very smoothly. No more major insults were hurled. We all agreed that we needed to work on our attitude toward ourselves, each other, and the people in our lives. Later, something significant seemed to happen for all of us, and it was really brought out by Dorothy.

"It is very hard for me to sit here with people who I think know me well and admit that I don't like my life when I have spent the last twenty years convincing you that I'm fine with the way things are," Dorothy said, almost to the point of tears.

Shirley got up from where she was sitting on the floor, went over to Dorothy, and put her arms around her. Before I knew it, all of us were hugging each other and crying—it seemed as if we couldn't stop. We were really crying, not crocodile tears. I'm talking about the type of crying a woman does when she is in pain. Later, when the tears subsided, everyone was looking at me as if to say, "Now that you've brought us this far, don't leave us hanging." I was so full of emotion that when I finally did speak I could barely recognize my voice—it was like another person was talking.

"What we just went through is what I call an emotional breakthrough or revelation. I think we all realize that we have choices about how we live our lives. Through the crying, we let some of that pent-up emotion out," I explained.

Julia's next comment helped to further relieve the tension that had built up. "Girlfriend, the way you were crying, I thought your ass was having a breakdown or a new baby," she said while putting her arms around my shoulders. That was Julia's way of letting me know that she was teasing me again. I really didn't mind Julia's teasing, but I did tell myself that I would find out why it bothered Sheila so much. My elementary psychology course told me that it had something to do with her relationship with Barbara. From my perspective, the two of them had a very interesting and interdependent relationship.

It was almost ten-thirty, and we were dealing with a lot of heavy-duty stuff about ourselves and how we wanted to create an environment in our lives where we could be productive. We decided that, in our own way, we were all capable of doing more with our lives than we were presently doing. I wanted to close our first session on a positive note. So I asked them to play a game. The game was identifying successful women and telling why they admired the woman they selected. I instructed them to respect each other's selection and not to comment until everyone had finished.

Barbara was the first to respond. "I admire and respect Hillary Clinton because she is intelligent and very smooth on her feet under pressure. She would do a better job as president than Bill."

Dorothy ignored my instructions and poked fun by saying, "Just like an accountant. She wants to invest the money Hillary made off the stock market."

The look I gave Dorothy told her to stop and told the others not to even think about joining in on the fun.

Julia got the message and said, "I respect and admire Coretta Scott King. She mourned for Martin after he died, but she just kept right on trucking, establishing a name for herself. Now, she's over there in South Africa hanging out with Nelson Mandela. I respect the girl for going after the power. Take the power, girl." Julia could be so theatrical, but everyone in the room understood that there was some real self-revelation in the comments that Julia had just made.

"I admire Tina Turner. She is so sexy and rambunctious. Her sex appeal transcends all ages," Sheila said, looking around the room at everyone.

Barbara winked at Sheila and said, "You should know about that transcending all age group stuff, huh, Sheila?"

Barbara's comment must have been a private joke between the two of them because it went over the heads of everyone else in the room.

"Barbara Jordan for me. That sister girl had it going on in her day. Even after she got sick, she continued to share her knowledge with other people," I chimed in to add to the list.

Dorothy said, "Diana Ross. She fooled the world when she left the Supremes. She got tired of waiting on Barry Gordy's old tired behind and went off with her white boys and did her thing. I take my hat off to Diana Ross."

"I respect and admire Madame C. J. Walker," said Paula.

Before she could continue, Sheila interrupted. "Who the hell is that?"

"Madame Walker was one of the first, if not the first, truly successful black business women in the beauty business. She made a fortune in black hair and black hair products. Too bad you weren't around then, Miss Accountant, you could have handled her money," Paula said. We could all tell that Paula truly enjoyed educating us about this matter.

The last one to give the name of the person they admired was Shirley. She said, "I admire the hell out of Oprah Winfrey. Girlfriend got one of the best looking Negroes in America and the bitch's hair ain't never out of place. And last, but not least, she got the money. She got the money." Shirley, who is usually very reserved, got up and strutted like Oprah.

We were all doubled up with laughter by the time Shirley decided to stop performing. I said, "Now that the performance is over, this may be a good time for us to bring closure to our first session." I got no argument from anyone. I said, "We all picked some very powerful and interesting personalities to admire, didn't we?"

"Yes, we did. In a funny kind of way, these women have some traits in common," Sheila said, looking around the room for confirmation of her observation.

"Girlfriend, you got to enlighten me there. What in the living hell do Barbara Jordan and Tina Turner have in common?" Barbara asked, doing the Sapphire neck roll as she asked the question.

Sheila, Julia, and Paula were in a dead heat trying to get to the floor to respond. Sheila won out. She said, "Both women are 'come-back' women: they are very strong, determined women. After Tina ran away from old, tired, abusive Ike Turner, she came back with a dynamic force. Now the whole world is aware of her talents. Likewise, Barbara Jordan took her place on Capitol Hill only to be brought down by a debilitating disease. She fought back with ferocious determination and made a valuable contribution as an educator. Is that enough for you, Missy?"

Everyone was impressed and satisfied with Sheila's response. Once again I tried to bring closure to the session by saying, "If we look at the lives of all the women, we see a common thread. I also think that if we examine ourselves, we see behaviors in them that we may want to emulate. Personally, I think that none of the seven women saw themselves as victims of circumstances or events. They all had a vision about what they wanted to experience in life, and they took the high road to get there. Let's take a lesson from them and stop whining about being victims. We can choose to do whatever we want with our lives."

It was almost midnight and from looking around the room at my friends, no one seemed tired. I continued with my comments. "We have covered a lot of ground tonight. We have a better understanding of ourselves and how we interact with each other. We have examined our attitudes and how we have choices about the direction in life we want to take. The next step is for us to get past the barriers that may be interfering with our experiencing our lives to the fullest."

In true form, Julia would not let me have the last word. "Okay, Claudia, what you just said is all well and good, but just what am I supposed to do between now and next month when we get together?"

Before I could respond, Sheila said, "Change your attitude, for heaven's sake!"

"I just might do that, Miss 'Thang,' but you have to promise to do the same thing," Julia retorted as she and Sheila picked up their purses to leave.

It was almost one o'clock before I finally got to bed. I was still very excited about what we had accomplished. I exhaled deeply and went to sleep with a smile on my face.

Session Two

I decided to use the first few minutes of our second session to let the ladies vent about what happened during the last month. After we talked about our workout sessions, someone observed how much more serious we had become since we started the support group. We were intent on making the fitness activities work effectively. We didn't play as much as we had before we had the first session at my house. Dorothy was particularly intense as she performed her exercises. She moved backward and forward on the equipment with renewed interest. All of us were self-conscious about our weight—several of us for good reason.

Personally, I could stand to lose about twenty pounds (okay about thirty). I guess I do a fairly good job of concealing my extra baggage. As a college professor, I can get away with a variety of nontraditional outfits and fashions that camouflage. I do a lot with African prints and other flowing tops so people don't see the bulges. Most people would truly be surprised to know that I was more than twenty pounds overweight.

Julia is a perfect size ten; she wears a lot of fitted suits and looks good in them. If she gains a pound or feels she is getting a Kellogg pinch, she starves herself and gets back in shape.

I would put Dorothy at about two hundred pounds. She dresses very smart. She is very self-conscious about her weight and has been for some time. Like the rest of us, she was trying on-again, off-again diets. This time around, she seemed very preoccupied with making this one work. When I talked with Shirley earlier in the week, she told me that Dorothy had missed one day at the gym and had called in sick the next day. Concerned about her, Shirley and Paula had gone to Dorothy's house to check on her. The cleaning lady told them that Dorothy was at the gym and had been there since early in the morning. They found out later that Dorothy had stayed at the gym all day trying to make up the time she had missed the day before.

Barbara and Sheila are about the same size. I put them at about ten to fifteen pounds overweight. They wear a lot of stylish suits tailored to complement their size. Many of their suits are made by a very good seamstress. One time I accompanied them on a fitting and I was truly surprised to see the real size of both of the ladies. They wear their weight well. While we were at the seamstress, Barbara discovered that her suit was a little snug. She said, "I wish I was not such a big-boned person." Sheila said, "I wish I did not have so much big meat around my bones." Both of them had a positive attitude toward their weight. From my perspective, their excess pounds did not seem to bother them.

At the second session, all of us were trying to talk at once except Sheila, who was pulling a wrapped dish from her oversize purse. When she uncovered it, the conversation halted.

"And just what do you think you are doing?" demanded Barbara.

"I told you that Claudia would not have any food, so I'm getting ready to eat my dessert. My goodness, the more I am around you guys, the more I am reminded that y'all need to get a life and give me mine. Doesn't it look like I'm about to eat? Pardon me if I did not ask permission."

"It looks like you are being disrespectful to Dorothy. You know she can't say no to sweets," Barbara said, looking disapprovingly at Sheila.

Dorothy spoke up, "That's okay, Sheila. I have decided that I have to take charge of my own demons. Isn't that what you called them the last time, Claudia?"

"Yes, that is what I called them, but how do you feel? Maybe I was wrong not to fix some stuff, I just thought—" I tried to ramble on.

Dorothy did not let me finish. She interrupted me, speaking very deliberately. "I'm not going to lie. Yes, I do feel that I want the dessert. But I want to get rid of these fifty or sixty pounds more than I want the dessert. I also have a confession to make. Paula and Shirley, my confession is really to the two of you. When I called in, I was not sick the other day. I had 'pigged out' the day before. I was so stuffed that I spent the entire next day in the gym. Can you imagine it? I spent more time in the gym in one day than I did the entire last year."

Neither Paula nor Shirley told Dorothy that they already knew what she had done.

I felt we were really coming together as a group. More importantly, I felt like real progress was ahead for us. I exhaled, feeling that the principles we discussed during our first session were already in action.

I decided to use this second session as a way for all of us to examine our personal paths to achievement. Even though we have known each other for over twenty years, there were still things we were not completely comfortable discussing with each other. I initiated the discussion by telling them about the topics we would cover during the course of the evening.

"I want to tell you guys something. You are really a beautiful bunch of women."

"Oh shit, we must really be going to wade through some heavy stuff tonight. Anytime Miss Thang starts off complimenting us, she has something up her sleeve," Julia said teasingly.

"Claudia can't help it. She is one deep sister, always serious. Always got her stuff together," Shirley said.

"Stop kissing up to the teacher, Shirley. You're still going to have to do the lesson, just like everyone else," Dorothy said, pretending to sound like a young child.

"Seriously, ladies. Tonight I want us to pick up where we left off last month. I'm sure, since then, each of us in our own way has started to examine ourself. Now it's time for us to probe deeper and see if we can get a handle on what may be standing in our way or path to personal achievement and fulfillment."

"I told you, ladies. Didn't I tell you that sister girl was going to come at us with both barrels? She has had a whole month to develop her game plan," Julia continued with her teasing.

Ignoring Julia's tease, I said, "Like I said, tonight we will look at barriers standing in our way, goals we may want to establish for ourselves, how to eliminate excess baggage, how to develop relationships with the right people, and how to remain focused on our goals."

"I did not bring my overnight bag. Why didn't you tell me we were having a weekend sleepover. Ain't no way we are going to cover all that tonight," Dorothy said, genuinely concerned.

"We can too, if we have one boss lady. The rest of you guys need to cooperate more and let Claudia conduct the business. She knows what she is doing," Sheila said.

"And the rest of us are stupid, Ms. Expert?" Julia asked in an irritated tone.

"If the shoe fits, wear it," Sheila said, giving Barbara the high-five sign.

Barbara responded weakly to the gesture. "Sheila, that was uncalled for. We do not need that. If we are going to be productive, we definitely do not need it. As you all can see, we have a long way to go to get the barriers out of our way. It goes without saying that there is no quick fix to what we are trying to do."

"I, for one, would like to get on with the discussion. I am ready to talk about them barriers you were talking about, but you don't have to throw baby girl out of the room," Dorothy said jokingly while bumping her shoulder affectionately up against Julia.

"Thanks, Dorothy, for getting us focused. Would you all buy into the fact that the biggest and most destructive barriers come from within ourselves? That barriers to success are really things we control ourselves? The big three are apathy, procrastination, and negativity," I said, hoping to inspire some dialogue.

"I can believe it and buy into it," said Paula.

"What if you have all three? At different times, I can truthfully say, I represent all of the things you just mentioned, Claudia," Dorothy responded.

"You guys, I don't think Claudia meant for all of us to go off the deep end because we see a few traits that we don't like. At least I hope not," Julia said, looking at me for affirmation.

"Exactly, Julia. You are right on the money. We have to be patient with ourselves. The three things I mentioned are big dream killers. Remember, we said we would look at personal things—things we could do something about. We can't accomplish everything at once. Let's take some small steps," I said, looking first at Julia and then around the room at the rest of the group. Everyone looked relaxed again. I wondered why we could be so negative toward each other at times. I was pleased that we were able to resolve our differences and get back on track with our session.

"Can we talk about negativity and how we can avoid it? This may be hard for you guys to realize or accept, but sometimes there is so much negativity going on in my house, I could just pick up and walk and not look back. But I can't and I don't," Paula said.

"I didn't know it was that bad. You're always so happy-go-lucky and outgoing," Dorothy said.

"Got to keep up that front, sister girl, got to keep up that front," Paula said, putting her hands over her eyes.

We all knew she was crying, but no one said a word. The silence was overwhelming. Dorothy was the first to move over to Paula. She put her arms around her and told her to let it out. After a few moments, Paula spoke.

"You guys go ahead and talk. Don't let me stifle what we have going on here. You see, when I got married, I decided it was for life. I know I love my husband. I love my children. But David has just gotten so negative in the last few years. I don't know him any more," Paula said.

"You have got to decide what you want. It seems to me that you have to find a way to either deal with the situation at home or get away from it," Sheila said.

"She done told you that she can't get away from it. Sometimes the people around us don't even know they are making us miserable. I ought to know," Dorothy said.

"Dorothy, I swear sometimes you really come out of left field. How in the world can somebody make you miserable and don't even know they are doing it?" Julia asked, frowning and confused.

"Now, that you ought to know, girlfriend. 'Cause you are good at making people miserable and I know you don't know. 'Cause if you did you would change, now wouldn't you?" Sheila challenged Julia to respond.

"Stop clowning, Sheila. This is serious conversation," Barbara said in a firm voice. Surprisingly, Sheila responded and did not give Barbara any lip.

"I don't want out of my relationship. I love David; I just want the warmth and passion back. I want the relationship to be the way it used to be," Paula said.

I could tell she was in a lot of pain when discussing her marriage. But she seemed to have the desire to let go of her feelings.

"This may be a good time for all of us to focus on our relationships and where we want to go in life. Are we headed in the direction we want to go? Or are we just following other people?" I said to get some of the pressure off Paula and to provide an arena for the others to share. I didn't realize that I was really opening the door for an even deeper disclosure.

Barbara uncharacteristically provoked Sheila. "Yea, Sheila. Are we following our own mind or are we being led by someone else?"

"Why don't you let me explain my business, Barbara? I know where you are trying to go with this discussion and it will not work. If you got something on your mind, stop beating around the bush. Don't come at me like that, girl. I won't stand for it and you know it."

Everyone was surprised by the heat in the conversation between Barbara and Sheila. No one spoke. I felt I needed to say something but, like the others, I had gotten caught up in the tension too.

"Okay, I will spit it out because I'm tired of covering for you; I'm tired of watching you make a fool of yourself. I can't believe that you would jeopardize your family by going with that young child," Barbara said, almost screaming at Sheila.

"He may be a child to you, but to me he is the best thing that has happened in my life in a long time. Since my big-mouth sister-in-law has put it out there, I am having an affair with a man ten years younger than me. I robbed the cradle according to you know who. So there! Satisfied Barbara? Are you satisfied now that you have embarrassed me in front of everyone?" Sheila said with a sigh of relief one can experience only after getting rid of a heavy load of emotions.

By now, both Sheila and Barbara were crying. The rest of us were so quiet we could hear ourselves breathe.

Sheila regained her composure. Barbara apologized to her and to the group for revealing a confidence. She said that she had no right to bring up something that personal about Sheila. I believe that everyone understood Barbara's intent but also recognized that the subject was so personal that Sheila should have been the one to bring it up if the group was going to be privy to the information. I was glad that we were starting to establish some ground rules on how we would share information and our feelings with each other.

"Well, Sheila, what do you intend to do?" Paula inquired.

"I don't know, but since we both seem to be in bad relationships, maybe the group here can help us sort through this madness," Sheila said.

"I don't think so, Sheila. I think we will have to work this one through for ourselves. For me, I'm going to take a long, hard look at what I want. Claudia, what was that you said earlier about goals?" Paula asked, giving me a perfect opportunity to talk about the subject.

I did feel that Paula was right—that if she and Sheila, and all of us for that matter, truly focused on our own personal goals, we could see what was in our lives that we needed to sort out. I thought this would be a good time to get the group to talk about goals, so I moved the conversation in that direction.

"How many of you made goals for this year?" I asked, and no one said a word. I continued, "All of you did. Remember, that is how we started this group—we all decided that we wanted to do something different and more productive with our lives. Tonight, we are going to take this idea one step further. We are going to write down our goals on paper."

"Claudia, are you taking this too far now? What good will it do for us to sit here tonight and put some scribble on paper?" Shirley asked, sounding genuinely confused.

"It won't do any good just to put some scribble on paper, but it will do some good if we put our personal goals on paper and monitor their completion," I responded, trying to put things into perspective.

"Personally, I like the idea of writing the goals down and sharing with you guys. Then I will have the six of you supporting me to see if I do them," Julia commented in support of what I had said. Julia was a very bright woman and frequently reminded others of her talents. I guess that is why she irritated this group sometimes. In confidence, Julia once told me that the only reason she tolerated the group was because of her friendship with me. At times, she was capable of demonstrating to us that she thought she was much smarter than anyone else in the group. What Julia did not know was that everyone else was aware of her attitude and was proud of her accomplishments.

"Then I know you will accomplish them, Julia, because you will never let anyone in this room, or anywhere else for that matter, outdo you," Shirley said.

"I will not argue with you there. I am just that way. I love competition," Julia said, smiling and doing her familiar sister girl neck roll.

"Julia is right. Sharing goals with each other can be very helpful if we are serious. Now everyone should take a break here and write their goals down. Then before we go home tonight we can share with each other," I instructed, hoping I could get them to complete the task before they changed their minds.

After our break, I asked everyone to share their goals. There was a long silence. The group was not talking. Everyone just sat around looking at each other.

"What is wrong? Before we broke, you guys were talkative. Now your mouths are shut up tight as Fort Knox. What's up?"

"I am not sure I want all of you to know what my goals are. Having you guys know my business could end up being too much pressure for me right now," Sheila said and obviously reflected what appeared to be the general attitude of everyone else because no one contradicted her.

"My idea for the next part of the session was to get all of you to really focus on your goals and where you want to go in life. I sense that this is not a good time for us to move in that direction. Let's talk about it. I can go either way."

It did not take us long to reach an agreement that we would not share with each other during this session. After a brief discussion, we decided that it was more important for us to concentrate on our goals in private instead of trying to share with each other at this time.

I was a little surprised to learn that my friends were also having some difficulty getting their thoughts down on paper. It was uncomfortable for me personally because a long time had passed since I had thought about what I wanted to do with my life.

Our compromise position was that we all would insert a list of our goals into envelopes and leave them with me for a few months. At a mutually agreed upon time, the envelopes would be opened and we would evaluate our success in reaching our goals. We also decided that instead of sharing the ideas with each other, we would just initiate our plans and then demonstrate what we had decided to do through our behavior over the next several months or year.

Session Three

For weeks now I have been trying to get the "magnificent seven" together. That is the name Paula started calling us a few weeks ago at the gym. We had experienced a tremendous workout and during a quick round of discussions in the parking lot outside the gym, Paula was the one to bring up the subject of how great we were looking these days. It was also the day that we decided that we all needed to get back together again. "Hey, you sisters is one magnificent sight to behold. Do y'all know we have kept ourselves together for over six months? Take a look at Claudia's butt. She is almost as fine as me and Julia. And get a load of Dorothy—no more 'heavy D' for her behind. Go on girl." Paula was in rare form that day, performing like a rap singer.

I realized that what Paula was saying was true. It was almost July, and we had started meeting over six months ago. Personally, I had dropped from a size fourteen to a size ten dress. I am not sure how much, but Dorothy had dropped significantly too. The bottom line is that she looked really good. Sheila, Barbara, and Shirley had mature bodies when we got started six months ago, but they had also gotten rid of their sweet-potato-pie pinch. Paula and Julia were our black Barbie dolls. I think those sisters could still fit in their high school cheerleader outfits. I found them both disgustingly slim in an admiring kind of way. I think that the only transformation for Julia and Paula was to their vanity and arrogance. Now they wait for someone else to tell them that they are beautiful instead of announcing it themselves.

When I left the group at the gym that night, Paula's comments replayed like a tape in my mind. I was very proud of us. For one thing, the fact that we had stayed together on our project for six months was nothing short of a miracle in itself. My mother used to tell me that to get more than two black folks to do something constructive together for more than one day was a major accomplishment. Well, today I was very excited about our accomplishments and was growing more curious by the hour about what was contained in the goal envelopes my friends had left in my care a few months before.

I had thought about opening the envelopes on many occasions. I tried everything (short of opening them) to see what my friends had written down as goals. I held the envelopes up to the light, and once I even got one of my daughter's old microscopes to see if I could penetrate the envelopes enough to discern what was written there. But my mother also told me it was wrong to open other folks' mail. (How much of my mother's advice had I followed anyway? If she were alive, she would probably say I had not followed much, but come to think of it, I seem to be following more of her advice now than I did when she was alive.)

After considerable effort but little gain with my surreptitious attempts to open my friends' envelopes, I decided to focus on my own goals instead of worrying about everyone else's. Finally, I picked up the telephone and called a man whom I needed to talk to about the rest of my life. The time had come to see if there was still a possibility for me to salvage my marriage.

It was a hard task getting the group back together after missing several months. I believe the reason was because of the high level of sensitivity surrounding our last meeting. It was okay for us to see each other in the gym. There, we could just fool around. But at our discussion groups, we were constantly dealing with very personal issues and hard-core concerns. I guess we needed some time away from each other before we could be ready to deal with the directions we wanted to take in our lives. At least we needed the time to see if we wanted to share with each other.

In between our meetings at the gym, I did try to stay in contact with the group as best I could. I really wanted to see if my friends were remaining focused on the goals they had listed for themselves. I am so competitive that checking on my friends helped me stay focused on my own goals. (There was no way I was going to let them achieve their goals and leave me behind.) It was interesting to observe that by helping other people, I also came out a winner.

Fascinating stuff came out of my follow-up with my friends. I found out that Dorothy had gone to Arizona to a fat farm for two weeks. It was expensive but it worked for her. Julia had joined a singles group and suddenly became very close-mouthed about her dating habits. She had also become less egotistical. For Julia, this was really obvious because ordinarily she is so blatant with her ego-driven image.

I noticed the change in Julia last week at lunch. I asked for her opinion about a fabric I was considering using for my couch and love seat. I was in the process of redecorating my bedroom and living room. You see, I had become very serious about making changes not only outside and inside, but also around myself.

The fabric I was looking at was a mud-cloth type of fabric. Julia told me that she liked the fabric very much. She did not stop there; she went on to tell me what else I should do to the entire house to make it more ethnic looking. According to Julia, my house needed a little more cultural flavor. Trust me, Julia was not the person to give advice about culture in the home. The only thing black in Julia's town house was a very expensive imported black bedroom set. From my point of view, it was too perfect to sleep on. So I interrupted my friend as she went off on her tangent about the decorations. "Julia, I know you are an expert at a lot of things, but I am going to leave the redecorating to my interior designer. All I wanted was a simple yes or no or nod of your head about the mud-cloth."

Julia, quick as always and in her most lawyer-like voice, said, "See there, see there, you mischaracterized me again.

Not to worry though, I forgive you. Just for your information, girlfriend, I am not the only expert around. Our dear friend Paula is also an expert. She steps in when I'm off duty. Julia was so proud of her sarcastic response that she jumped up and did a copycat Michael Jackson moon walk. She looked silly doing that jig in her form-fitted suit that only Barbie dolls can wear and look good in no matter what they are doing. We left the restaurant laughing. I have no doubt that the other guests in the restaurant thought we were crazy.

I did have a difficult time keeping in contact with Paula. Every time I called her, she was not in. Her son would inform me that she and David were out at a meeting.

I was able to maintain limited contact with Shirley and Dorothy. Every time I talked with them, except when we were at the gym, they were whispering about some business deal they were working on.

It was easy making contact with Barbara and Sheila. Follow the dollar and there they were, making money and making more money using other people's money.

So almost four months after the last group session, here we were again, but certainly not the way we were six months ago. My aim during this session was to get the group to open those goal envelopes! I did not care to go through another month of waiting to see what everyone had written.

I started the meeting by asking the ladies to give an update of what was happening in their lives—and to come clean with the information in the goal envelopes. Full disclosure was what I asked for.

After the usual small talk, I said, "Why don't we just go around the room and share anything that is happening in our lives that we want each other to know about."

"David and I are going to counseling," Paula blurted out almost before I could complete my statement. "I finally confronted him with my suspicions about his outside relationships. At first, he shined me on. Then he finally confessed that he was seeing one of the girls at his office. You know it hurts, but not as much as it did when I first heard about it."

"What happened then?" Dorothy insisted.

"We started talking about it. He told me that he did not like our lifestyle and that we were moving much faster than he wanted to travel. After I stopped pouting and blaming myself for the problems, I got plenty angry at David and the chippie he was fooling around with. One day a couple of months ago, I even swallowed my pride and went down to David's office and stood outside across the street until his girlfriend came out," Paula said and then suddenly stopped talking and looked around the room at us. She seemed to be trying to determine if we were listening.

"Oh no you don't! She ain't stopping there," Sheila jumped up from her chair and went over to where Paula was sitting. "Girlfriend, if you want to leave here in one piece, you best get to telling the rest of the story."

"Go ahead, Paula, tell us what she looked like. Was she fine or was homeboy messing around with Aunt Sheba's daughter?" Julia chimed in with her usual sarcasm.

Paula jumped up, went to the center of the room, dropped her head and said, "Well, she ain't ugly, but she can't touch this. She can't touch this," pointing at herself and acting like M. C. Hammer in his prime.

When Paula finally stopped performing, she told us that she and David were going to counseling and were now experiencing a newfound closeness in their relationship.

I noticed that Dorothy and Shirley were grinning widely while Paula was talking. They were both chomping at the bit to talk. At first, I thought they had some provocative insight for Paula, but when they finally got the floor, what they said was completely different from what I had expected.

"Shirley and I have something to say and it also involves Paula, only she does not know about it," Dorothy said.

"You guys know how many years I have wanted to have my own business. You guys also know how Shirley, Paula, and I are the backbones behind Hair-R-Us beauty school, right? Well about two months ago, Shirley and I heard about the white beauty school downtown going out of business. Probably too many of our rowdy cousins were enrolling in the school. But that ain't what I really want to tell you."

"Get to the point, Dorothy. Give us the short version," Julia interrupted impatiently.

"Okay, Miss Thang. Shirley and I, well, we investigated and found out that it was really true. The white school was getting ready to close down." Recognizing that the rest of us wanted her to get to the point too, Dorothy started talking extra fast.

"Barbara and Sheila looked into the financing for us, and we have come up with a business plan. The bank has approved our loan, and we are now the owners of the beauty salon and school," Dorothy finished, smacking her lips like she used to do after eating a piece of my mama's sweet potato pie. I could tell from her delight that telling us about the deal was sweeter than any piece of pie any of us could ever cook up. I got goose pimples just watching her excitement.

I was about to go on to someone else, but Dorothy stopped me. "Not so fast, Claudia. Shirley needs to tell you the rest of the story."

I sat back and said, "Go on then. Excuse me for stopping the progress."

"We decided to do this business stuff right, so we called Paula's husband at the construction company to help us. At first, we were trying to get some help from our family, but some of them got really funny when we started talking about finances. One of my brothers started talking about his stock and other stuff that did not have anything to do with him investing money with us," Shirley said, stopping to take a deep breath.

The rest of us could tell that Paula did not know about this because her look telecasted, "My David?"

Reading her mind, Shirley continued, "Yes, your David. He and his crew have been working day and night to get Three Sisters Hair Design up and running for a grand opening, just in time for the Christmas holidays." Shirley, getting into one of her scripture-quoting moods, said, "My cup runneth over. Surely goodness and mercy will follow me all the days of my life. Hallelujah. Ain't God wonderful?"

Everyone in the room joined in her exclamation in unison. "Yes, she is!"

I got caught up in the mix. I was just sitting there watching my beautiful friends. We really were a magnificent group. Sheila was the next person to speak.

"I have some information to share. I guess you could say my message is both good and bad. It really depends on how you look at it. Barbara and I have some joint news, so I'll let her tell you about that later. Now, I want to tell you about me. I have left Troy. We're getting a divorce. I will no longer live a lie of trying to live two lives. I've done that for five years now and it is too heavy. I may as well come clean in one big swoop. I will be getting remarried as soon as the divorce is final. Brent will stay with Troy."

"Isn't this rather sudden?" Julia inquired, not able to resist the lawyer instinct. The rest of us looked on in shock.

"No, it is not, Julia. I've thought about it too hard and for too long. Brent will be fine with Troy. All of you guys know that child was born grown. He knows exactly what he wants to do with his life. He wants to be a doctor. He saves every penny he gets his hands on. He probably has his first allowance from elementary school."

Under her breath, Barbara commented, "Wonder where he picked up that habit?"

Sheila continued. "I plan to marry Donald Richardson in December. I see all of your faces. No, I am not crazy. I've been crazy but I ain't crazy now. For once in my life I am doing what I want to do with my life. I am giving myself one big Christmas present. A new husband! I know I cannot expect your approval of what I am doing. I will settle for your understanding. You guys know things have not been right between me and Troy for a long time."

Feeling that Sheila needed some visible sign of support (her voice had started to crack), I said, "Sheila, we will be there for you. We understand what you are going through."

Julia almost bit my head off. "Well, I, for one, do not understand one iota of what sister girl is talking about. She has it going on! The house, the car, the bankroll, the man who is together working hard to make things right for her, and she's willing to give it up for a young lay! No matter how you shake or bake it, I can't begin to fathom what she is doing. It just ain't fair!"

"Fair to whom, Julia? We are not talking about you. We are talking about Sheila. I think she has a right to live her life the way she calls it. To hell with public opinion. She doesn't need people second guessing her. And she certainly does not need it from someone who has not been able to maintain a decent relationship in the past ten years. Why don't you take the fifth on this one counselor," Barbara came back fiercely in Sheila's defense.

Sheila started to talk again, oblivious to the storm that had just brewed up between Barbara and Julia. "Things have not been right between Troy and me since I lost the baby a few years ago. He simply did not forgive me. When I had the miscarriage, he said that had I stayed home instead of working so hard, we would have a baby girl today. Did I ever tell you guys the baby I lost was a girl? Well, right after losing the baby, both Troy and I started working more. We made more money to buy things. It was during this time that I met Donald and he literally became a refuge for me. Then I fell in love with him. Donald touched my soul. He was recently divorced. We were both running from something we did not want to face," Sheila finished on a very sad note.

"How can you do this to Troy and Brent? You are one piece of shit. I can't believe the rest of you are sitting here listening to this crap without telling Sheila she is tripping. And you call yourself friends. With friends like you guys, I would just as soon ask my enemies for advice," Julia snapped at the rest of us without any compassion in her voice.

Shirley said, "Julia, you are the one that is tripping. How would you like to be trapped in a meaningless relationship?"

Before Julia could speak, Paula blurted out, "Trapped is the only way Miss Thang will ever get anybody to stay in a relationship with her. Julia knows she's out to lunch on this and that Sheila has the right to free herself."

"Julia cannot have any compassion for Sheila because something bigger than friendship is in her eyes. But I'm not going there. The attorney needs to investigate herself and get off Sheila's case," Barbara commented, her words going over everybody's head. Julia looked defiantly at Barbara but did not comment back. That was unusual for Julia. She never backed away from an argument.

"Julia, you are wrong about the lay part. I admit that may be the way we started off. But it is much more than that. Troy has known about my relationship with Donald for over two years. Of course, I did not know that he was aware of it until a few months ago. When I first talked with Troy about the divorce, he told me that he already knew and that he was relieved I was involved with someone else. He said he no longer had an interest or desire to be a real husband to me."

Dorothy said, "That is so sad. Here I was thinking you guys were the perfect couple."

"You thought that because that is what you wanted to see. I bet when you think about it, during the last ten years, did you ever see any passion between me and Troy?"

"Sheila, get a grip. You are old enough to know you are messing up a good thing and for the life of me, I don't know why," Julia replied.

"And for the life of me, girlfriend, I think it is time that you check your attitude toward Sheila," Barbara said, deliberately challenging Julia to step out of place.

Sheila resumed her story. She had a lot to say and the rest of us were her captive audience.

"Troy said I could keep the relationship with Donald but just don't embarrass him in public. Can y'all imagine how that made me feel? Well, when I decided to stop hating myself, I moved out and then made up my mind to get the divorce. You guys can help me though. Troy wants to keep up the front. If he doesn't change his attitude, things could get messy in the future."

"And they are not now?" Julia asked sarcastically.

"I am not going to change my mind. I have lived the last forty years trying to fit into an image that was not me. I plan to use the next forty differently. I hope my friends will understand and accept that. The rest of the world? Well, I could care less," Sheila said, looking at Julia in a very defiant way.

There was a very pregnant pause before Barbara spoke.

"I am ready to tell you guys about another topic. We definitely need to change the subject before I roll Miss Thang all over Claudia's floor in her two thousand dollar suit," Barbara said, throwing a menacing look at Julia. Then she continued. "Shirley and Dorothy told you about the financing package we did for them. You know white folks, when one of them makes a dollar, the rest of them can smell it and they will milk that cow. Or in our case two black cows. Our accounting firm got so many calls about the deal we did for Three Sisters that Sheila and I are practically celebrities in the financing business. The company now wants Sheila and me to head up a small business development division. In other words, we decided to let them milk us and we will moo all the way to the bank."

Sheila nodded her head, approving of what Barbara was saying.

Barbara spoke up again. "I want to say to Sheila in front of all of you how terribly sorry I am for not doing more to see her pain. I am sorry that I was so absorbed in my life that I did not even bother to deal with your pain. I was so busy working my agenda with you that I did not even acknowledge yours."

Paula said, "Well, since I am going through my own little personal crisis, I have a lot of empathy for Sheila. Anything I can do, Sheila, just let me know and I will be there."

Barbara, on the verge of tears, got back in the discussion. "I guess I wanted you to stay in your little box so I would not have to get out of mine. Sheila, can you ever forgive my selfishness?"

Julia, steaming like a teapot getting ready to blow the whistle, said, "Who is the selfish one here? Little Miss Adulteress is the selfish one! She is willing to throw away twenty years of quality life. For what? Beats me. You guys are really pitiful. This stuff is simply too heavy for me. I need a break."

"There you go again making fun of somebody else's misery. Julia, you need to grow up. Why are you so opinionated? You are the selfish, shallow one, not Sheila. You may have that law degree behind your name, but when God handed out the common sense, you must have been in the rest room somewhere. You are the pitiful one, not Sheila. What is sad about the whole thing is that you don't even know you are pitiful," Dorothy retaliated, shaking her head.

Julia jumped up and did her famous neck roll, went quickly over to Dorothy and said, "Listen holier than thou. I don't need this stress. I am out of here. You guys can stay here and play make believe with each other. I am out of here!" She picked up her purse and left, slamming my front door so hard that my chandelier rocked.

The rest of us just sat there looking at each other. Before anyone could say anything, Julia was back in the room. "Since you have been so obliging with your opinion about me, Miss Dorothy, I want to take a few minutes to give you a piece of my mind. All of you are sitting around here criticizing me. You need to look at yourselves. I'm here to tell you something. I earned my damn attitude the hard way. Nobody sent Julia's behind to law school. I know what it is like to work in the hot sun until you're so tired you wish you would faint so you would not have to keep on working. Yea, I earned my attitude and there ain't much about me that I want to change. I like my life the way it is. I guess if I had to, I would change my love life. But listening and watching you here tonight, I'm not sure I want what you guys have!"

Dorothy chimed in. "Julia, why don't you just run an ad in the personals for Mr. Perfect or why not just marry yourself? You're probably the only person on the face of the earth good enough for you."

"No, I don't have to do that. I joined a singles group of black professionals."

"I do not believe you Julia. Where did you get your list, *Black Enterprise's* top 100 businessmen?" Shirley asked mockingly.

"No, I got my list from *Forbes* and *Inc.* Maybe I'll get jungle fever like Claudia. It seems to be working for her."

"Julia, why are you always messing with Claudia about her husband? Do you want the man for yourself?" Sheila asked.

"No, hell no. That ain't it at all. Claudia knows what time it is. I deal with Claudia because she gets on my nerves trying to masquerade in front of you guys about being Miss Black Doris Day. Little Miss Claudia has messed up two, maybe three good lives just because she does not have the courage to fess up to the fact that she loves her 'own-self' husband whose only crime is that he came into this world a white man. She has got her daughter so messed up that she is identityless—if that is a word. Everybody just tiptoes around Claudia 'cause they don't want to hurt her little feelings. I love the sister enough to call a spade a spade. I love her enough to tell her the truth. She needs to change that tune. Get real, girlfriend, and stop me when I lie on you,"

Julia said, looking dead in my eyes, inviting me to deny what she had just said.

"Wait just a minute, Julia, don't even go there. Talk about me like you do all the time, but leave my daughter and my husband out of it!" I lost it and screamed at Julia.

"What part of what I said is a lie, Claudia? Tell us what part?"

"Jacqueline has her own identity. She just refuses to let race or anyone define her. She is handling her business the way she wants to. She has her own independent relationship with her father. We both like it that way," I responded defensively.

Julia would not leave me alone. "Isn't the real reason you can't be with your husband for any length of time is because you are ashamed of your feelings for him? Don't you think your daughter can see through you? Isn't that why you hide Jack out when he comes to town? Claudia, you know as well as I do that's the reason Jackie went so far away. She wanted to get away from your hypocritical behind so that she could be free to have her own relationship with her father," Julia said in closing argument form. When she finished talking, she stood up, arms folded, defying me to defend myself.

"Julia, you are doing all the telling," I said, sounding feeble and not at all defiant. I knew that everyone in the room realized that Julia had finally crossed the line with me. But I was no match for Julia in this arena. I just sat there like a junkyard dog without a bone.

No one had to tell me that I had lost control of the group. Try as I might for the rest of the evening, I could not get everyone back to talking about our goals. No one seemed to make eye contact with me for the rest of the evening.

We made small talk for a few minutes after my tit for tat with Julia. Finally, everyone left with weak excuses about having to get up early the next day.

I tried to recap in my mind what I could have done differently that evening. I decided that it really did not matter what any one of us said or did. I did regret that I did not have the chance to share with the group what was happening in my life since our last meeting. That fact alone caused me to think hard about what Julia had said to me. The big concern I had was how much of what she had said was really true. It was early morning before I was able to fall asleep. The sounds of garbage collectors working outside mixed with the silence of my tears lulled me into a deep sleep.

Session Four

Three weeks passed before I saw any of the magnificent seven again. I did talk with Julia on the telephone just before I left for Louisiana and Texas. We laid to rest our concerns about the last meeting at my house. Julia apologized for embarrassing me before the group but maintained that she was not sorry about what she said. She told me that she still thought I had some unfinished business to take care of in the near future.

In Louisiana, I visited my daughter, Jacqueline, who was a medical student there. We had a great visit. I told Jacqueline what Julia had said about our relationship and the reasons Julia gave for her leaving home. According to Jacqueline, Julia was tripping.

"Mom, Aunt Julia knows you better than anyone else in this world minus me and Pops. Next to us, she's also the person who loves you the most. She's been talking about your crossover personality or split personality ever since I can remember. But woman, you know she loves you and wants you and Pops together. After all, she takes credit for introducing the two of you. Do you know what really has Aunt Julia bent out of shape?"

Julia and I had been so close over the years that Jacqueline referred to her as her aunt even though Julia and I were not blood related.

"Yes, I do," I said, lying to my own daughter.

"She can't stand the idea about being wrong about you and Pops. It is really killing her that you two are not together. Aunt Julia hung the moon—she is so smart. How could a simple transaction like planning your and Pop's life go so wrong for her?" Jacqueline said, mimicking Julia's famous neck roll.

"No. No. No. You see, you are wrong. Julia just admitted to me recently that she did not hang the moon by herself. She had an assistant."

"Yeah, right, but the fat lady has not sung yet when it comes to you and my father. As an expert witness, I think Aunt Julia made a good match. You two will be back together before I am out of medical school."

"Well, if you take much longer we will be forced to live back with each other to cut costs to have money to pay your tuition," I said, teasing my daughter, knowing that part of what I said was true. She was taking a long time to finish because she was having a difficult time with some of her classes. She had not shared this with me. Her father had told me during one of our recent conversations.

Jacqueline was her father's daughter all the time and mine some of the time. She identified with him so much when she was a little girl that she had her friends call her Jac. When people would telephone the house and ask to speak to Jack, Jacqueline would inquire, "Jack the man or the girl?"

Jack insisted on paying all of Jacqueline's fees for medical school. Quite frankly, I was relieved, but I was also concerned that I was not making much of a contribution to my daughter's adult development and education. Jack says he likes being able to do it because he wasn't there much for Jacqueline during the formative years. I accepted the arrangement because it made it possible for both of us to share our daughter.

Before I left Louisiana, Jacqueline poked her nose into my business. She asked me if it was true that I was planning to visit her father in Dallas after my visit with her. When I told her that I was, she gave me some solid daughterly advice.

"Mom, when are you going to stop the yo-yo with Pops? Either love him or let him go. He'll never get a life as long as you keep popping in and out. And you won't have a real one either. Both of you are getting too old for that shit. Well, maybe I'm getting too old. I would like to see what it is like to have just one Christmas instead of two before I turn fifty."

"Thanks for the free advice, Missy."

"You're welcome. Kiss my old man when you see him. Oh, by the way, Aunt Julia knows you are not at the NAACP convention in Dallas. She said she knew the convention was in Minneapolis this year."

I don't know why I lied to Julia about visiting my husband in Dallas. Maybe I was getting back at her for the things she said to me at the last meeting at my house. The better part of the truth is that I was still confronting myself and had not quite realized what I wanted to do with my personal life.

When I returned from Dallas, I rounded up the magnificent seven. I told them to come to a meeting at my house, or I would open up those envelopes without them and print the contents in the newspaper.

When everyone arrived, I distributed the envelopes. My instructions to my friends were either to tell what was in the envelope or read it, but more importantly evaluate whether the goals had been reached or not.

I personally felt that we had come a long way since January. Looking around the room, it was clear that each person had made some major progress since that first meeting. Even the living room in which we were meeting had undergone a major face-lift.

Reflecting back on that first night when we were trying to understand ourselves as women, I don't think any of us had confidence in our abilities to transform the way we actually did over the last few months. That night back in January, we had a very hard time just focusing on the topic. While we were comfortable being ourselves, we wanted to grow as individuals. However, we really had not given much consideration to the fact that we had the power to change our own lives. But by the time we made it to our second or third session, we started to deal with ourselves and each other. At first, it was difficult to break away from some of our old habits such as mistreating ourselves and each other. We lashed out at each other, but we worked through the tough spots and finally got focused on making positive changes in our lives.

As I reflected on our walk to self-discovery, I remember going into the spring. We were just beginning to get rid of our self-destructive attitudes and remove some of the stumbling blocks from our paths. It took us a long time to look at our personal goals. In the process, we even had to test and retest each other. There was quite a bit of dumping on ourselves and each other. I guess you could call that growing pains.

By early summer, we were getting focused on our personal selves and interests. We finally reached the point that we were ready to look at personal goals. We wrote them down on paper and put them in envelopes.

Tonight, almost one year later, we were sitting where we started the walk and were ready to open the envelopes and share those goals. As we sat there looking at each other holding on to those envelopes, one might have thought we were holding the envelopes at the Academy Awards and the winners were being announced.

In a strange sort of way, I guess the Academy Award is a pretty good analogy because on this night we were the stars and opening the envelopes would determine whether we had won or not. The following is the revelation of what those important envelopes contained for each of us.

Barbara

What She Wrote

Within the next six months or year, I plan to be more of my own person. I intend to get out of Sheila's shadow and demonstrate my own talents. In addition to making other people rich, it is my desire to get my own piece of the pie. And that family of mine. They will understand that I have needs and desires too. I'm going on a really good vacation with my husband. We will lock the door behind us and throw away the key. No kids. No work or business. Just us.

What She Did

Barbara and Sheila masterminded a small business plan for Dorothy, Paula, and Shirley. The plan was so successful that the firm they worked for started a small business development division. Barbara was promoted to vice president. She also positioned herself to leverage for stock in the company. She took that vacation with her husband and no doubt threw away the key—she is now expecting a child. Maybe she'll use the money from her promotion to hire a nanny to help with the kids.

Sheila

What She Wrote

I know exactly what I should do six months from now. I need to do what pleases me. They [the group] would be shocked to know my real feelings. I am so tired of this game. I am tired of these sessions. I am tired of being trapped. I want to be able to be myself again. In six months, I hope I have the backbone to tell my husband that I want a divorce and just keep walking, thinking about nothing but my new life.

What She Did

Sheila did get control of her life. She and Barbara developed a small business plan for Dorothy and Shirley. The plan helped both Sheila and Barbara get promotions. Sheila refused the promotion with the existing company and got a transfer to San Francisco where she is able to do what she does best—make money for other people. Sheila made other changes in her life. She divorced her husband and remarried soon thereafter. Her new husband, Donald, is about ten years younger than she is. Sheila believes that the age difference will help keep her young.

Dorothy

What She Wrote

If another one of them calls me "heavy D" again, I am going off the deep end. I am a very sexy woman and my face is much prettier than all of theirs. I could go on a program and lose weight and I'll be okay. But look at them: they need all of that makeup and then some to look better than me. If I have to spend every dime I have during the next few months, I'm going to get this weight off and show them what a real woman looks like. Just because I'm not a big mouth like Julia or "kiss everybody's behind" like Claudia doesn't mean I don't have feelings. In six months, I'm going to be as bad as I wanna be.

What She Did

Dorothy was true to her word. She took off the pounds. First to show the rest of the group. And then to show herself. She did spend a considerable amount of money as she declared she would. Dorothy went to a fat farm and did extra duty in the gym. She would exercise with the group and then secretly go to the gym again on her own. Her husband became her personal trainer, and she now enjoys a renewed friendship and relationship with him. Dorothy is also one of the new owners of Three Sisters Hair Design. She and her husband are working on a fitness video for large sisters, not Barbie dolls. Dorothy discovered that many of the videos on the market seem to be for people who are already in shape and not designed for people trying to get to the ideal weight. She and her husband, Jim, decided to undertake this project because when Dorothy was in the gym alone, she felt so self-conscious about her size. They decided that large women should not have to experience the discomfort of working out with people looking down their noses at them.

Shirley

What She Wrote

I ought to be able to make this money from the divorce work for me. But I know I cannot do it myself. If Paula was not so busy running after that husband of hers and Dorothy was not so busy feeling sorry for herself because of her size, I could talk some real business with them. God will help those that help themselves. He said seek and thee shall find. I am certainly going to seek a way to stop letting other people pimp me. I know that I am not coveting anyone else's possessions. But there ought to be a way black folks can start owning their own businesses. During the next six months, I will spend every daylight hour I can to find a way to get a business of my own started. I am going to talk some sense into Dorothy and Paula if it is the last thing I do.

What She Did

Shirley went to Dorothy with her idea about branching off and starting a business. Dorothy jumped on the idea enthusiastically. Paula was going through a really bad time with her home life. Sheila and Dorothy decided to approach Paula's husband with the idea. He joined in to help them without Paula's knowledge. Sheila and Barbara worked out the financing. Paula's share in the business was contributed by her husband in the form of sweat equity. He did the renovation of the beauty salon at no charge. The cost of the labor was tallied and constituted Paula's investment as the third owner of the Three Sisters Hair Design. Shirley was the primary investor and owns 50 percent of the building with Paula and Dorothy as equal partners for the other fifty percent. Shirley still has no personal love interest. She says that for the next several years, she will be married to the salon. She does not make any apologies for being a workaholic; it works for her. Shirley said that she will feel sorry for herself all the way to the bank.

PAULA

What She Wrote

I don't ask much of the world. I could be happy if I just could get to the bottom of what is keeping my husband from loving me right. I know it ain't my looks because I still look good for a thirtysomething woman. The only person that comes close to looking as good as me in this group is Julia. But her face comes up short. Within the next six months, I am going to get to the bottom of what is eating at my old man. I think he is cheating on me. If I find out that it is true, he will regret the day he was born. I'm not afraid of a little competition, but I will be damned if I am going to sit around and let some other woman walk off with my life or my future. I'm up to the challenge. I may be a small piece of leather, but I'm well put together. Now I just got to make him think so.

What She Did

Paula confirmed her suspicions. Her husband was cheating on her. He confessed after she confronted him. They started going to counseling together. Paula checked the competition. She concluded that the woman her husband was seeing was no match for her. She and her husband experienced a new romance in their lives. He even helped her become a partner in the business with her coworkers, Dorothy and Shirley. Paula and Julia still compete as to who is the fairest of them all. They both vote for themselves; they both win.

Julia

What She Wrote

Next year will not find me a single woman. I will have a real man in my life if I have to send applications out to my friends. This group here could help me, but they are far too selfish. They will not help me find a good man because if they do, I will be doing better than them. They are so selfish that way. Anyway, I probably would not like the man they would pick out for me. It is not like any of them picked a Denzel Washington. Claudia is so pitiful; she messed up with the one I picked for her. Anyway, come next year this time, I will have a man of my own or borrow someone else's. I will not be by myself. Today, I am looking for Mr. Right, but if I run out of time, I will settle for Mr. Adequate. I am not kidding.

What She Did

Julia joined a singles group. She was very secretive about it for a long time. She met a businessman in the group. He and Julia found that they had a lot in common. Both enjoyed talking about themselves. The man that she met was attractive to look at and dressed almost as well as Julia. He was also very ambitious. Although she did not appear to be emotionally attached to him, she seemed to enjoy dating him as a friend.

She has also started to date Sheila's ex-husband. Well that went over like a lead balloon among the magnificent seven. It bothered everyone else more than it did Sheila. When you think about it, Julia and Troy made a good match—they were both very ambitious and liked a lot of the black aristocratic events. Troy and Julia both started to teach at the university—Troy in the medical school and Julia at the law school. He likes to dress well and travel and so does Julia.

When Sheila first told us that she was leaving Troy, Julia was her worst critic. Now it seems that she is the most elated member of the group. Frankly, I'm glad to see Julia with a good man. My grandmother used to say, "A good man is like an expensive cologne. They don't wear the same on every woman." From the outside looking in, Julia seems to be quite comfortable with the way Troy was wearing on her. We can only guess what the final effect will be on the group.

Me/Claudia

What I Wrote

During the next year I am going to develop an acute case of "me-ism." I am going to get my body tuned up. I want to look good in a pair of jeans with a white shirt tucked inside. I am going to repossess my husband, if he will have me. It may be good to express myself the way I want to, reflecting my own aspirations. I am going to walk the rainbow—I will not even wait to exhale.

What I Did

You already know that I bugged the members of the magnificent seven to meet and go through our transformations as we walked our personal rainbows. You know I went to the gym with the rest of the group. I lost weight. I dropped four dress sizes. Through all of my teenage years and young adult life, I have struggled to avoid a matronly appearance because of my thunder thighs. Finally, I got fed up enough to do something about it. I went to a plastic surgeon and got rid of those thighs. Now I have the hips of a twenty-five year old. I am as bad as I wanna be and looking real good in those jeans. My doctor told me he took almost five pounds off each of those thighs.

My husband? When I tried to repossess him, I found out that it would not be that easy. He said he would give me a second chance, but on his own terms. Jacqueline is also helping by playing cupid. Jack is making me pass a few tests before he decides if he wants to get back in the fold permanently. I know he still loves me, and I finally admitted that he is the only man for me. The test I have to pass in a few weeks is that I have to take Jack to an NAACP meeting, sit in the front row, and hold his hand. He doesn't know it, but I'm looking forward to it. It is not a problem because I know who I am now.

One last thing I did was to take notes on my observations and conversations with my friends during our sessions over the last few months. Why did I do that? I wrote this book so I could share it with you. Enjoy your walk over the rainbow. Don't wait to exhale. Do it and do it now!

Epilogue

The way I see it, for much of our lives, African American women have relied on the opinions of others to shape our lives. Whether we admit it or not, we also held others responsible for our lives.

Walk the Rainbow was created to show you how to take that responsibility from other people and place yourself in the position of authority and responsibility over your own life. Designing your own plan to walk the rainbow will empower you to exhale and use your abilities to take control of your life.

Your faith in yourself is the key to staying focused on what you want from life. Decide early what is valuable to you, and if what is in front of you has no value for you, simply do not accept it. You have the right to reject meaningless intrusions. Make sure that the activities you plan to engage in are appropriate to your goals before undertaking them.

Remember, you are the star and producer of your life script. Do not assign these roles to others. Only you can ultimately decide what your final goals will be in life. Anything you allow into your life should enhance your well-being and happiness.

In this book I encouraged you to develop and use a number of empowerment tools so that your life can be rich and fulfilling. I hope you will use these ideas as you walk the rainbow in pursuit of your pot of gold.

ORDER FORM

If you know someone who would benefit from ***Walk the Rainbow—When You Get Tired of Waiting to Exhale***, you can order more copies of this book by filling out the following information.

Please send _____ copies of ***Walk the Rainbow*** to

(Please Print)

NAME ____

ADDRESS ____

CITY ______________________________ STATE ______ ZIP ______________

Cost: Single copy $12.95 $ ___________

California sales tax: ___________

Postage & handling: $3.50 ___________
(for 1 to 3 books)

TOTAL ENCLOSED: $ ___________

Please send check or money order to:

Sido-Mari Publishing
5267 Warner Avenue, #152
Huntington Beach, CA 92649
Phone: 714-846-3017
Fax: 714-846-7245

To have Dr. Johnson speak to your organization or conduct a workshop, please call, write or fax to the above address and phone numbers.